Thomas Jefferson
Still
Survives!

Thomas Jefferson Still Survives!

Thomas Jefferson, in his own words, speaks out on Life, Liberty, and the Pursuit of Happiness

Edited by Mike Thorsen

Writers Club Press
San Jose New York Lincoln Shanghai

Thomas Jefferson Still Survives!
Thomas Jefferson, in his own words, speaks out on Life, Liberty, and the
Pursuit of Happiness

Writers Club Press
an imprint of iUniverse.com, Inc.

For information address:
iUniverse.com, Inc.
5220 S 16th, Ste. 200
Lincoln, NE 68512
www.iuniverse.com

ISBN: 0-595-19580-6

Printed in the United States of America

Dedicated to Life, Liberty, and the Pursuit of Happiness.

EPIGRAPH

I have sworn upon the altar of God, eternal hostility against every form of tyranny over the mind of man.

—Thomas Jefferson

Contents

FOREWORD

Of all the founding fathers of the United States of America, it is probably Thomas Jefferson who has had the most enduring effect. Most everyone knows him as the author of the American Declaration of Independence and the third President, but few know him as, probably, the greatest legal mind in American history and our greatest architect of limited, but effective, government. A reading of this volume will demonstrate his credentials for these claims.

In spite of his fame and the enormity of his political and private writings, Thomas Jefferson is still probably one of the most misunderstood and most misquoted Americans. One of the aims of this volume was to clear up these misconceptions and put forth his opinions, in his own words, on popular topics in an easily accessible format. Thereby, a reader can look up Term Limits and find that Jefferson, indeed, was for them; or look up Exercise and find that he believed that staying in shape was important for happiness; or read Jefferson's opinion on George Washington. "Thomas Jefferson Still Survives!" can be used a reference volume or a good read. Either way, the reader should enjoy this book.

"Thomas Jefferson Still Survives!" was undertaken in the belief that Thomas Jefferson still has enormous wisdom to offer modern day America. As he predicted, America has deviated from our "republican tact" and needs some work to get back on track. Thomas Jefferson, I believe, can provide that wisdom.

Thomas Jefferson died July 4, 1826 on the 50th anniversary of the Declaration of Independence. His friend, John Adams died later that same day. Adams' dying words were, "The republic is safe for Thomas Jefferson still Survives!".

EDITORIAL METHOD

All words in the book are Thomas Jefferson's. However, in an effort to make the text more readable, the spelling and punctuation has been updated and exerts were edited to fit within the topical nature of the book.

CHRONOLOGY

Thomas Jefferson

1743 (April 13) Born in Albemarle County, Virginia.

1772 (January 1) Married Martha Wayles Skelton.

1776 Wrote the Declaration of Independence.

1779 Elected Governor of Virginia.

1782 Mrs. Martha Jefferson died.

1785 Appointed Minister to France.

1789 Became Secretary of State.

1797-1801 Vice-President of the United States.

1801-1809 President of the United States.

1819 Founded the University of Virginia.

1826 (July 4) Died at Monticello, Virginia.

AMERICAN CHARACTER

It is a part of the American character to consider nothing as desperate to surmount every difficulty by resolution and contrivance. In Europe there are shops for every want: its inhabitants therefore have no idea that their wants can be furnished otherwise. Remote from all other aid, we are obliged to invent and to execute; to find means within ourselves, and not to lean on others.

[Letter to Martha Jefferson, Aix-en Provence, March 28, 1787]

ARISTOCRACY

I agree with you that there is a natural aristocracy among men. The grounds of this are virtue and talents. Formerly, bodily powers gave place among the aristoi. But since the invention of gunpowder has armed the weak as well as the strong with missile death, bodily strength, like beauty, good humor, politeness and other accomplishments, has become but an auxiliary ground of distinction. There is also an artificial aristocracy, founded on wealth and birth, without either virtue or talents; for with these it would belong to the first class. The natural aristocracy I consider as the most precious gift of nature, for the instruction, the trusts, and government of society. And indeed, it would have been inconsistent in creation to have formed man for the social state, and not to have provided virtue and wisdom enough to manage the concerns of the society. May we not even say, that that form of government is the best, which provides the most effectually for a pure selection of these natural aristoi into the offices of government? The artificial aristocracy is a mischievous ingredient in government, and provision should be made to prevent its ascendancy.

[Letter to John Adams, Monticello, October 28, 1813]

CENSORSHIP

I am really mortified to be told that, "in the United States of America", a fact like this can become a subject of inquiry, and of criminal inquiry too, as an offence against religion; that a question about the sale of a book can be carried before the civil magistrate. Is this then our freedom of religion? And are we to have a censor whose imprimatur shall say what books may be sold, and what we may buy? And who is thus to dogmatize religious opinions for our citizens? Whose foot is to be the measure to which ours are all to be cut or stretched? Is a priest to be our inquisitor, or shall a layman, simple as ourselves, set up his reason as the rule for what we are to read, and what we must believe? It is an insult to our citizens to question whether they are rational beings or not, and blasphemy against religion to suppose it cannot stand the test of truth and reason. If M. de Becourt's book be false in its facts, disprove them; if false in its reasoning, refute it. But for God's sake, let us freely hear both sides, if we choose.

[Letter to Monsieur N.G. Dufief, Monticello, April 19, 1814]

CITIZENSHIP

And shall we refuse the unhappy fugitives from distress that hospitality which the savages of the wilderness extended to our fathers arriving in this land? Shall oppressed humanity find no asylum on this globe?

[First Annual Message, December 8, 1801]

CONFORMITY

It is a singular anxiety which some people have that we should all think alike. Would the world be more beautiful were all our faces alike? were our tempers, our talents, our tastes, our forms, our wishes, aversions and pursuits cast exactly in the same mould? If no varieties existed in the animal, vegetable or mineral creation, but all move strictly uniform, catholic and orthodox, what a world of physical and moral monotony it would be! These are the absurdities into which those run who usurp the throne of God and dictate to Him what He should have done. May they will all their metaphysical riddles appear before that tribunal with as clean hands and hearts as you and I shall. There, suspended in the scales of eternal justice, faith and works will show their worth by their weight.

[Letter to Charles Thomson, Monticello, January 29, 1817]

CONSOLATION

I have the consolation to reflect that during the period of my administration not a drop of the blood of a single fellow citizen was shed by the sword of war or of the law, and that after cherishing for eight years their peace and prosperity I laid down their trust of my own accord and in the midst of their blessings and importunities to continue in it. But, beginning to be sensible of the effect of age, I feared that its infirmities might injure their interests and believed the example would be salutary against inveteration in office, and I now enjoy in retirement the comfort of their good will and of a conscience calm and without reproach.

[Letter to Count Dugnani, Monticello, February 14, 1818]

THE CONSTITUTION

To make us one nation as to foreign concerns, and keep us distinct in domestic ones, gives the outline of the proper division of powers between the general and particular governments. But, to enable the federal head to exercise the powers given it to best advantage, it should be organized as the particular ones are, into legislative, executive, and judiciary. The first and last are already separated. The second should be. When last with Congress, I often proposed to members to do this, by making of the committee of the States, an executive committee during the recess of Congress, and, during its sessions, to appoint a committee to receive and dispatch all executive business, so that Congress itself should meddle only with what should be legislative. But I question if any Congress (much less all successively) can have self-denial enough to go through with this distribution. The distribution, then, should be imposed on them.

[Letter to James Madison, Paris, December 16, 1786]

How do you like our new constitution? I confess there are things in it which stagger all my disposition to subscribe to what such an Assembly has proposed. The house of federal representatives will not be adequate to the management of affairs, either foreign or federal. Their President seems a bad edition of a Polish King. He may be elected from four years to four years, for life. Reason and experience prove to us, that a chief magistrate, so continuable, is an office for life. When one or two generations shall have proved that this is an office for life, it becomes, on every occasion, worthy of intrigue, of bribery, of force, and even of foreign interference. It will be of great consequence to France and England, to have America governed by a Galloman or Angloman. Once in office, and possessing the military force of the Union, without the aid or check of a council, he would not be easily dethroned, even if the people could be induced to withdraw their votes from him. I wish that at the end of the four years, they had made him forever ineligible a second time. Indeed, I think all the good of this new constitution might have been couched in three or four new articles, to be added to the good, old and venerable fabric, which should have been preserved even as a religious relic.

[Letter to John Adams, Paris November 13, 1787]

Let me add, that a bill of rights is what the people are entitled to against every government on earth, general or particular; and what no just government should refuse, or rest on inference. The second feature I dislike, and strongly dislike, is the abandonment, in every instance, of the principle of rotation in office, and most particularly in the case of the President.

I own, I am not a friend to a very energetic government. It is always oppressive. It places the governors indeed more at their ease, at the expense of the people....And say, finally, whether peace is best preserved by giving energy to the government, or information to the people. This last is the most certain, and the most legitimate engine of government. Educate and inform the whole mass of the people. Enable them to see that it is their interest to preserve peace and order, and they will preserve them. And it requires no very high degree of education to convince them of this. They are the only sure reliance for the preservation of our liberty. After all, it is my principle that the will of the majority should prevail. If they approve the proposed constitution in all its parts, I shall concur in it cheerfully, in hopes they will amend it, whenever they shall find it works wrong.

[**Letter to James Madison, Paris December 20, 1787**]

I hope, therefore, a bill of rights will be formed, to guard the people against the federal government, as they are already guarded against their State governments, in most instances. The abandoning the principle of necessary rotation in the Senate, has, I see, been disapproved by many; in the case of the President, by none. I readily, therefore, suppose my opinion wrong, when opposed by the majority, as in the former instance, and the totality, as in the latter.

[**Letter to James Madison.<@151>Paris, July 31, 1788**]

On similar ground it may be proved, that no society can make a perpetual constitution, or even a perpetual law. The earth belongs always to the living generation: they may manage it, then, and what proceeds from it, as they please, during their usufruct. They are masters, too, of their own persons, and consequently may govern them as they please. But persons and property make the sum of the objects of government.

The constitution and the laws of their predecessors are extinguished then, in their natural course, with those whose will gave them being. This could preserve that being, till it ceased to be itself and no longer.

Every constitution, then, and every law, naturally expires at the end of thirty-four years. If it be enforced longer, it is an act of force, and not of right. It may be said, that the succeeding generation exercising, in fact, the power of repeal, this leaves them as free as if the constitution or law had been expressly limited to thirty-four years only.

In the first place, this objection admits the right, in proposing an equivalent. But the power of repeal is not an equivalent. It might be, indeed, if every form of government were so perfectly contrived, that the will of the majority could always be obtained, fairly and without impediment. But this is true of no form. The people cannot assemble themselves; their representation is unequal and vicious. Various checks are opposed to every legislative proposition. Factions get possession of the public councils, bribery corrupts them, personal interests lead them astray from the general interests of their constituents; and other impediments arise, so as to prove to every practical man, that a law of limited duration is much more manageable than one which needs a repeal.

[Letter to James Madison, Paris, September 6, 1789]

Our citizens, however, should derive from this some useful lessons. They should see in it a necessity to rally firmly and in close bands round their Constitution. Never to suffer an iota of it to be infringed.

[Letter to William Bache, Philadelphia, February 2, 1800]

Some men look at constitutions with sanctimonious reverence, and deem them like the Ark of the Covenant, too sacred to be touched. They ascribe to the men of the preceding age a wisdom more than human, and suppose what they did to be beyond amendment. I knew that age well; I belonged to it, and labored with it. It deserved well of its country. It was very like the present, but without the experience of the present; and forty years of experience in government is worth a century of book reading; and this they would say themselves, were they to rise from the dead. I am certainly not an advocate for frequent and untried changes in laws and constitutions. I think moderate imperfections had better be borne with; because, when once known, we accommodate ourselves to them, and find practical means of correcting their ill effects. But I know also, that laws and institutions must go hand in hand with the progress of the human mind. As that becomes more developed, more enlightened, as new discoveries are made, new truths disclosed, and manners and opinions change with the change of circumstances, institutions must advance also, and keep pace with the times. We might as well require a man to wear still the coat which fitted him when a boy, as civilized society to remain ever under the regimen of their barbarous ancestors.

It is this preposterous idea which has lately deluged Europe in blood. Their monarchs, instead of wisely yielding to the gradual change of circumstances, of favoring progressive accommodation to progressive improvement, have clung to old abuses, entrenched themselves behind steady habits, and obliged their subjects to seek through blood and violence rash and ruinous innovations, which, had they been referred to the peaceful deliberations and collected wisdom of the nation, would have been put into acceptable and salutary forms.

Let us follow no such examples, nor weakly believe that one generation is not as capable and another taking care of itself, and of ordering its own affairs. Let us, as our sister States have done, avail ourselves of our reason and experience, to correct the crude essays of our first and unexperienced, although wise, virtuous, and well-meaning councils. And lastly, let us provide in our Constitution for its revision at stated periods.

What these periods should be, nature herself dictates. Each generation is as independent of the one preceding, as that was of all which had gone before. It has then, like them, a right to choose for itself the form of government it believes most promotive of its own happiness; consequently, to accommodate to the circumstances in which it finds itself, that received from its predecessors; and it is for the peace and good of mankind, that a solemn opportunity of doing this every nineteen or twenty years should be provided by the Constitution; so that it may be handed on, with periodical repairs, from generation to generation, to the end of time, if anything human can so long endure.

[Letter to Samuel Kercheval, Monticello, July 12, 1816]

These are rights which it is useless to surrender to the government, and which governments have yet always been found to invade. These are the rights of thinking, and publishing our thoughts by speaking or writing; the right of free commerce; the right of personal freedom.

There are instruments for administering the government, so peculiarly trust-worthy, that we should never leave the legislature at liberty to change them. The new Constitution has secured these in the executive and legislative department; but not in the judiciary. It should have established trials by the people themselves, that is to say, by jury. there are instruments so dangerous to the rights of the nation, and which place them so totally at the mercy of their governors, that those governors, whether legislative or executive, should be restrained from keeping such instruments on foot, but in well-defined cases. Such an instrument is a standing-army.

We are now allowed to say, such a declaration of rights, as a supplement to the Constitution where that is silent, is wanting; to secure us in these points. The general voice has legitimated this objection. It has not, however, authorized me to consider as a real defect, what I thought and still think one, the perpetual re-eligibility of the President. But three States out of eleven, having declared against this, we must suppose we are wrong, according to the fundamental law of every society, the *lex majoris partis*, to which we are bound to submit. And should the majority change their opinion, and become sensible that this trait in their Constitution is wrong, I would wish it to remain uncorrected, as long as we can avail ourselves of the services of our great leader, whose talents and whose weight of character I consider as peculiarly necessary to get the government so under way, as that it may afterwards be carried on by subordinate characters.

[**Letter to Colonel Humphreys, Paris, March 18, 1789**]

I do then, with sincere zeal, wish an inviolable preservation of our present federal Constitution, according to the true sense in which it was adopted by the States, that in which it was advocated by its friends, and not that which its enemies apprehended, who therefore became its enemies; and I am opposed to the monarchising its features by the forms of its administration, with a view to conciliate a first transition to a President and Senate for life, and from that to an hereditary tenure of these offices, and thus to worm out the elective principle.

[Letter to Elbridge Gerry, Philadelphia, January 26, 1799]

I approved, from the first moment, of the great mass of what is in the new Constitution; the consolidation of the government; the organization into executive, legislative, and judiciary; the subdivision of the legislative; the happy compromise of interests between the great and the little States by the different manner of voting in the different Houses; the voting by persons instead of States; the qualified negative on laws given to the executive, which, however, I should have liked better if associated with the judiciary also, as in New York; and the power of taxation. I thought at first that the latter might have been limited. A little reflection soon convinced me it ought not to be.

What I disapproved from the first moment also, was the want of a bill of rights, to guard liberty against the legislative law as well as the executive branches of the government; that is to say, to secure freedom in religion, freedom of the press, freedom from monopolies, freedom from unlawful imprisonment, freedom from a permanent military, and a trial by jury, in all cases determinable by the laws of the land. I disapproved, also, the perpetual re-eligibility of the President. To these points of disapprobation I adhere. My first wish was, that the nine first conventions might accept the constitution, as the means of securing to us the great mass of good it contained, and that the four last might reject it, as the means of obtaining amendments. But I was corrected in this wish, the moment I saw the much better plan of Massachusetts, and which had never occurred to me.

With respect to the declaration of rights, I suppose the majority of the United States are of my opinion; for I apprehend, all the anti-federalists and a very respectable proportion of the federalists, think that such a declaration should now be annexed. The enlightened part of Europe have given us the greatest credit for inventing the instrument of security for the rights of the people, and have been not a little surprised to see us so soon give it up. With respect to the re-eligibility of the President, I find myself differing from the majority of my countrymen; for I think there are but three States out of the eleven which have desired an alteration of this. And indeed, since the thing is established, I would wish it not to be altered during the life of our great leader, whose executive talents are superior to those, I believe, of any man in the world, and who, alone, by the authority of his name and the confidence reposed in his perfect integrity, is fully qualified to put the new government so under way, as to secure it against the efforts of opposition. But, having derived from our error all the good there was in it, I hope we shall correct it, the moment we can no longer have the same name at the helm.

[Letter to Francis Hopkinson, Paris, March 13, 1789]

In the arguments in favor of a declaration of rights, you omit one which has great weight with me; the legal check which it puts into the hands of the judiciary. This is a body, which, if rendered independent and kept strictly to their own department, merits great confidence for their learning and integrity. In fact, what degree of confidence would be too much, for a body composed of such men as Wythe, Blair and Pendleton? On characters like these, the *civium ardor prava jubentium.* ("The wayward zeal of the ruling citizens.") would make no impression. I am happy to find that, on the whole, you are a friend to this amendment. The declaration of rights is, like all other human blessings, alloyed with some inconveniences, and not accomplishing fully its object. But the good in this instance, vastly overweighs the evil. I cannot refrain from making short answers to the objections which your letter states to have been raised

That the rights in question are reserved, by the manner in which the federal powers are granted. Answer. A constitutive act may, certainly, be so formed, as to need no declaration of rights. The act itself has the force of a declaration, as far as it goes, and if it goes to all material points, nothing more is wanting. In the draught of a constitution which I had once a thought of proposing in Virginia, and printed afterwards, I endeavored to reach all the great objects of public liberty, and did not mean to add a declaration of rights. Probably the object was imperfectly executed; but the deficiencies would have been supplied by others, in the course of discussion. But in a constitutive act which leaves some precious articles unnoticed, and raise implications against others, a declaration of rights becomes necessary, by way of supplement. This is the case of our new federal Constitution. This instrument forms us into one State, as to certain objects, and gives us a legislative and executive body for these objects. It should, therefore, guard us against their abuses of power, within the field submitted to them.

A positive declaration of some essential rights could not be obtained in the requisite latitude. Answer. Half a load is better than no bread. If we cannot secure all our rights, let us secure what we can.

The limited powers of the federal government, and jealousy of the subordinate governments, afford a security which exists in no other instance.

Answer. The first member of this seems resolvable into the first objection before stated. The jealousy of the subordinate governments is a precious reliance. But observe that those governments are only agents. They must have principles furnished them, whereon to found their opposition. The declaration of rights will be the text, whereby they will try all the acts of the federal government. In this view, it is necessary to the federal government also; as by the same text, they may try the opposition of the subordinate governments.

Experience proves the inefficacy of a bill of rights. True. But though it is not absolutely efficacious under all circumstances, it is of great potency always, and rarely inefficacious. A brace the more will often keep up the building which would have fallen, with that brace the less. There is a remarkable difference between the characters of the inconveniences which attend a declaration of rights, and those which attend the want of it. The inconveniences of the declaration are, that it may cramp government in its useful exertions. But the evil of this is short-lived, moderate and reparable. The inconvenience of the want of a declaration are permanent, afflicting and irreparable. They are in constant progression from bad to worse. The executive, in our governments, is not the sole, it is scarcely the principle object of my jealousy. The tyranny of the legislatures is the most formidable dread at present, and will be for many years. That of the executive will come in its turn; but it will be at a remote period. I know there are some among us, who would now establish a monarchy. But they are inconsiderable in number and weight of character. The rising race are all republicans. We are educated in royalism; no wonder, if some of us retain that idolatry still. Our young people are educated in republicanism; an apostasy from that to royalism, is unprecedented and impossible. I am much pleased with the prospect that a declaration of rights will be added, and I hope it will be done in that way, which will not endanger the whole frame of government, or any essential part of it.

[Letter to James Madison, Paris March 15, 1789]

Our situation is indeed perilous, and I hope my countrymen will be sensible of it, and will apply, at a proper season, the proper remedy; which is a convention to fix the constitution, to amend its defects, to bind up the several branches of government by certain laws, which, when they transgress, their acts shall become nullities; to render unnecessary an appeal to the people, or in other words a rebellion, on every infraction of their rights, on the peril that their acquiescence shall be construed into an intention to surrender those rights.

[Notes on Virgina]

To this state of general peace with which we have been blessed, one only exception exists. Tripoli, the least considerable of the Barbary States, had come forward with demands unfounded either in right or in compact, and had permitted itself to denounce war, on our failure to comply before a given day. The style of the demand admitted but one answer. I sent a small squadron of frigates into the Mediterranean, with assurances to that power of our sincere desire to remain in peace, but with orders to protect our commerce against the threatened attack. The measure was seasonable and salutary. The bey had already declared war in form. His cruisers were out. Two had arrived at Gibraltar. Our commerce in the Mediterranean was blockaded, and that of the Atlantic in peril. The arrival of our squadron dispelled the danger. One of the Tripolitan cruisers having fallen in with, and engaged the small schooner Enterprise, commanded by Lieutenant Sterret, which had gone as a tender to our larger vessels, was captured, after a heavy slaughter of her men, without the loss of a single one on our part. The bravery exhibited by our citizens on that element, will, I trust, be a testimony to the world that it is not the want of the virtue which makes us seek their peace, but a conscientious desire to direct the energies of our nation to the multiplication of the human race, and not to its destruction.

Unauthorized by the constitution, without the sanction of Congress, to go beyond the line of defense, the vessel being disabled from committing further hostilities was liberated with its crew. The legislature will doubtless consider whether, by authorizing measures of offence, also, they will place our force on an equal footing with that of its adversaries. I communicate all material information on this subject, that in the exercise of the important function confided by the constitution to the legislature exclusively, their judgment may form itself on a knowledge and consideration of every circumstance of weight.

[**First Annual Message, December 8, 1801**]

When an instrument admits two constructions, the one safe, the other dangerous, the one precise, the other indefinite, I prefer that which is safe and precise. I had rather ask an enlargement of power from the nation, where it is found necessary, than to assume it by a construction which would make our powers boundless.

Our peculiar security is in the possession of a written Constitution. Let us not make it a blank paper by construction. I say the same as to the opinion of those who consider the grant of the treaty making power as boundless. If it is, then we have no Constitution. If it has bounds, they can be no others than the definitions of the powers which that instrument gives. It specifies and delineates the operations permitted to the federal government, and gives all the powers necessary to carry these into execution. Whatever of these enumerated objects is proper for a law, Congress may make the law; whatever is proper to be executed by way of a treaty, the President and Senate may enter into the treaty; whatever is to be done by a judicial sentence, the judges may pass the sentence. Nothing is more likely than that their enumeration's of powers is defective. This is the ordinary case of all human works. Let us go on then perfecting it, by adding, by way of amendment to the Constitution, those powers which time and trial show are still wanting.

[Letter to Wilson C. Nicholas, Monticello, September 7, 1803]

The party called republican is steadily for the support of the present constitution. They obtained at its commencement, all the amendments to it they desired. These reconciled them to it perfectly, and if they have any ulterior view, it is only, perhaps, to popularize it further, by shortening the Senatorial term, and devising a process for the responsibility of judges, more practicable than that of impeachment. They esteem the people of England and France equally, and equally detest the governing powers of both.

[Letter to John Melish, Monticello, January 13, 1813]

CORRUPTION

Mankind soon learns to make interested uses of every right and power which they possess, or may assume. The public money and public liberty, intended to have been deposited with three branches of magistracy, but found inadvertently to be in the hands of one only, will soon be discovered to be sources of wealth and dominion to those who hold them; distinguished, too, by this tempting circumstance, that they are the instrument, as well as the object of acquisition. With money we will get men, said Caesar, and with men we will get money. Nor should our assembly be deluded by the integrity of their own purposes, and conclude that these unlimited powers will never be abused, because themselves are not disposed to abuse them. They should look forward to a time, and that not a distant one, when a corruption in this, as in the country from which we derive our origin, will have seized the head of government, and be spread by them through the body of the people; when they will purchase the voices of the people, and make them pay the price. Human nature is the same on every side of the Atlantic, and will be alike influenced by the same causes. The time to guard against corruption and tyranny, is before they shall have gotten hold of us. It is better to keep the wolf out of the fold, than to trust to drawing his teeth and claws after he shall have entered.

[**Notes on Virginia**]

THE DECLARATION OF INDEPENDENCE

—Thomas Jefferson's Original Version.

When in the course of human events, it becomes necessary for one people to dissolve the political bands which have connected them with another, and to assume among the powers of the earth the separate and equal station to which the laws of nature and of nature's God entitle them, a decent respect to the opinions of mankind requires that they should declare the causes which impel them to the separation.

We hold these truths to be self evident: that all men are created equal; that they are endowed by their Creator with inherent and inalienable rights; that among these are life, liberty, and the pursuit of happiness; that to secure these rights, governments are instituted among men, deriving their just powers from the consent of the governed; that whenever any form of government becomes destructive of these ends, it is the right of the people to alter or abolish it, and to institute new government, laying its foundation on such principles, and organizing its powers in such form, as to them shall seem most likely to effect their safety and happiness. Prudence, indeed, will dictate that governments long established should not be changed for light and transient causes; and accordingly all experience hath shown that mankind are more disposed to suffer while evils are sufferable, than to right themselves by abolishing the forms to which they are accustomed. But when a long train of abuses and usurpation's, begun at a distinguished period and pursuing invariably the same object, evinces a design to reduce them under absolute despotism, it is their right, it is their duty to throw off such government and to provide new guards for their future security. Such has been the patient sufferance of these colonies; and such is now the necessity which constrains them to expunge their former systems of government. The history of the present king of Great Britain is a history of unremitting injuries and usurpation's, among which appears no solitary fact to contradict the uniform tenor of the rest, but all have in direct object to the establishment of an absolute tyranny over these states. To prove this, let facts be submitted to a candid world for the truth of which we pledge a faith yet unsullied by falsehood.

He has refused his assent to laws the most wholesome and necessary for the public good.

He has forbidden his governors to pass laws of immediate and pressing importance, unless suspended in their operation till his assent should be obtained; and, when so suspended, he has utterly neglected to attend to them.

He has refused to pass other laws for the accommodation of large districts of people, unless those people would relinquish the right of representation in the legislature, a right inestimable to them, or formidable to tyrants only.

He has called together legislative bodies at places unusual, uncomfortable, and distant from the depository of their public records, for the sole purpose of fatiguing them into compliance with his measures.

He has dissolved representative houses repeatedly and continually for opposing with manly firmness his invasions on the rights of the people.

He has refused for a long time after such dissolution's to cause others to be elected, whereby the legislative powers, incapable of annihilation, have returned to the people at large for their exercise, the state remaining, in the meantime, exposed to all the dangers of invasion from without and convulsions within.

He has endeavored to prevent the population of these states; for that purpose obstructing the laws for naturalization of foreigners, refusing to pass others to encourage their migrations hither, and raising the conditions of new appropriations of lands.

He had suffered the administration of justice totally to cease in some of these states refusing his assent to laws for establishing judiciary powers.

He has made our judges dependent on his will alone for the tenure of their offices, and the amount and payment of their salaries.

He has erected a multitude of new offices, by a self-assumed power and sent hither swarms of new officers to harass our people and eat out their substance.

He has kept among us in times of peace standing armies and ships of war without the consent of our legislatures.

He has affected to render the military independent of, and superior to, the civil power.

He has combined with others to subject us to a jurisdiction foreign to our constitutions and unacknowledged by our laws, giving his assent to their acts of pretended legislation for quartering large bodies of armed troops among us; for protecting them by a mock trial from punishment for any murders which they should commit on the inhabitants of these states; for cutting off our trade with all parts of the world; for imposing taxes on us without our consent; for depriving us of the benefits of trial by jury; for transporting us beyond seas to be tried for pretended offenses; for abolishing the free system of English laws in a neighboring province, establishing therein an arbitrary government, and enlarging its boundaries, so as to render it at once an example and fit instrument for introducing the same absolute rule into these states; for taking away our charters, abolishing our most valuable laws, and altering fundamentally the forms of our governments; for suspending our own legislatures, and declaring themselves invested with power to legislate for us in all cases whatsoever.

He had abdicated government here by withdrawing his governors, and declaring us out of his allegiance and protection.

He has plundered our seas, ravaged our coasts, burnt our towns, and destroyed the lives of our people.

He is at this time transporting large armies of foreign mercenaries to complete the works of death, desolation and tyranny already begun with circumstances of cruelty and perfidy unworthy the head of a civilized nation.

He has constrained our fellow citizens taken captive on the high seas, to bear arms against their country, to become the executioners of their friends and brethren, or to fall themselves by their hands.

He has endeavored to bring on the inhabitants of our frontiers, the merciless Indian savages, whose known rule of warfare is an undistinguished destruction of all ages, sexes and conditions of existence.

He has incited treasonable insurrections of our fellow citizens, with the allurements of forfeiture and confiscation of our property.

He has waged cruel war against human nature itself, violating its most sacred rights of life and liberty in the persons of a distant people who never offended him, captivating and carrying them into slavery in another hemisphere, or to incur miserable death in their transportation hither. This piratical warfare, the opprobrium of INFIDEL powers, is the warfare of the CHRISTIAN king of Great Britain. Determined to keep open a market where MEN should be bought and sold, he has prostituted his negative for suppressing every legislative attempt to prohibit or to restrain this execrable commerce. And that this assemblage of horrors might want no fact of distinguished die, he is now exciting those very people to rise in arms among us, and to purchase that liberty of which he has deprived them, by murdering the people on whom he also obtruded them: thus paying off former crimes committed against the LIBERTIES of one people, with crimes which he urges them to commit against the LIVES of another.

In every stage of these oppressions we have petitioned for redress in the most humble terms: our repeated petitons have been answered only by repeated injuries.

A prince whose character is thus marked by every act which may define a tyrant is unfit to be the ruler of a people who mean to be free. Future ages will scarecely believe that the hardiness of one man adventured, within the short compass of twelve years only, to lay a foundation so broad and so undisguised for tyranny over a people fostered and fixed in principles of freedom.

Nor have we been wanting in attentions to our British brethren. We have warned them from time to time of attempts by their legislature to extend a jurisdiction over these our states. We have reminded them of the circumstances of our emigration and settlement here, no one of which could warrant so strange a pretension: that these were effected at the expense of our own blood and treasure, unassisted by the wealth or the strength of Great Britain: that in constituting indeed our several forms of government, we had adopted one common king, thereby laying a foundation for perpetual league and amity with them: but that submission to their parliament was no part of our constitution, nor ever in idea, if history may be credited: and, we appealed to their native justice and magnanimity as well as to the ties of our common kindred to disavow these usurpation's which were likely to interrupt our connection and correspondence. They too have been deaf to the voice of justice and of consanguinity and when occasions have been given them, by the regular course of their laws, of removing from their councils the disturbers of our harmony, they have, by their free election, re-established them in power. At this very time too, they are permitting their chief magistrate to send over not only soldiers of our common blood, but Scotch and foreign mercenaries to invade and destroy us. These facts have given the last stab to agonizing affection, and manly spirit bids us to renounce forever these unfeeling brethren. We must endeavor to forget our former love for them, and hold them as we hold the rest of mankind, enemies in war, in peace friends. We might have a free and a great people together; but a communication of grandeur and of freedom, it seems, is below their dignity. Be it so, since they will have it. The road to happiness and to glory is open to us, too. We will tread it apart from them, and acquiesce in the necessity which denounces our eternal separation.

We therefore the representatives of the United States of America in General Congress assembled, to in the name, and by the authority of the good people of these states reject and renounce all allegiance and subjection to the kinds of Great Britain and all others who may hereafter claim by, through or under them; we utterly dissolve all political connection which may heretofore have subsisted between us and the people or parliament of Great Britain: and finally we do assert and declare these colonies to be free and independent states, and that as free and independent states, they have full power to levy war, conclude peace, contract alliances, establish commerce, and to do all other acts and things which independent states may of right do.

And for the support of this declaration, we mutually pledge to each other our lives, our fortunes, and our sacred honor.

DIFFICULTIES

If ever you find yourself environed with difficulties and perplexing circumstances, out of which you are at loss how to extricate yourself, do what
is right, and be assured that that will extricate you the best out of the worst
situations. Though you cannot see, when you take one step, what will be
the next, yet follow truth, justice, and plain dealing, and never fear their
leading you out of the labyrinth, in the easiest manner possible. The knot
which you thought a Gordian one, will untie itself before you. Nothing is
so mistaken as the supposition, that a person is to extricate himself from a
difficulty, by intrigue, by chicanery, by dissimulation, by trimming, by an
untruth, by an injustice. This increases the difficulties tenfold; and those,
who pursue these methods, get themselves so involved at length, that they
can turn no way but their infamy becomes more exposed.

[Letter to Peter Carr, Paris, August 19, 1785]

DIVISION OF POWER

To make us one nation as to foreign concerns, and keep us distinct in domestic ones, gives the outline of the proper division of powers between the general and particular governments. But, to enable the federal head to exercise the powers given it to best advantage, it should be organized as the particular ones are, into legislative, executive, and judiciary.

[Letter to James Madison, Paris December 16, 1786]

The idea of separating the executive business of the confederacy from Congress, as the judiciary is already, in some degree, is just and necessary. I had frequently pressed on the members individually, while in Congress, the doing this by a resolution of Congress for appointing an executive committee to act during the sessions of Congress, as the committee of the States was to act during their vacations. But the referring to this committee all executive business, as it should present itself, would require a more persevering self-denial than I suppose Congress to possess. It will be much better to make that separation by a federal act. The negative, proposed to be given them on all the acts of the several legislatures, is now, for the first time, suggested to my mind. *Prima facie*, I do not like it. It fails in an essential character; that the hole and the patch should be commensurate. But this proposes to mend a small hole by covering the whole garment. Not more than one out of every hundred State acts concern the confederacy. This proposition, then, in order to give them one degree of power, which they ought to have, gives them ninety-nine more, which they ought not to have, upon a presumption that they will not exercise the ninety-nine.

[Letter to James Madison, Paris, June 20, 1781]

DUTY

My great wish is, to go on in a strict but silent performance of my duty; to avoid attracting notice, and to keep my name out of newspapers, because I find the pain of a little censure, even when it is unfounded, is more acute than the pleasure of much praise. The attaching circumstance of my present office, is, that I can do it duties unseen by those for whom they are done.

[Letter to Francis Hopkinson., Paris, March 13, 1789]

ECONOMICS

I think the war will not be short, because the object of England, long obvious, is to claim the ocean as her domain and to exact transit duties from every vessel traversing it. This is the sum of her orders of council, which were only a step in this bold experiment, never meant to be retracted if it could be permanently maintained. And this object must continue her in war with all the world. To this I see no termination, until her exaggerated efforts, so much beyond her natural strength and resources, shall have exhausted her to bankruptcy.

The approach of this crisis is, I think, visible in the departure of her precious metals, and depreciation of her paper medium. We who have gone through that operation, know its symptoms, its course, and consequences. In England they will be more serious than elsewhere, because half the wealth of her people is now in that medium, the private revenue of her money-holders, or rather of her paper-holders, being, I believe, greater than that of her land-holders. Such a proportion of property, imaginary and baseless as it is, cannot be reduced to vapor but with great explosion. She will rise out of its ruins, however, because her lands, her houses, her arts will remain, and the greater part of her men. And these will give her again that place among other nations which is proportioned to her natural means, and which we all wish her to hold. We believe that the just standing of all nations is the health and security of all.

[Letter to James Maury, Monticello, April 25, 1812]

I have not formerly been an advocate for great manufactories. I doubted whether our labor, employed in agriculture, and aided by the spontaneous energies of the earth, would not procure us more than we could make ourselves of other necessaries. But other considerations entering into the question, have settled my doubts.

[Letter to John Melish, Monticello, January 13, 1813]

Like a dropsical man calling our for water, water, our deluded citizens are clamoring for more banks, more banks. The American mind is now in that state of fever which the world has so often seen in the history of other nations. We are under the bank bubble, as England was under the South Sea bubble, France under the Mississippi bubble, and as every nation is liable to be, under whatever bubble, design, or delusion may puff up in moments when off their guard.

We are now taught to believe that legerdemain tricks upon paper can produce as solid wealth as hard labor in the earth. It is vain for common sense to urge that *nothing* can produce but *nothing*; that it is an idle dream to believe in a philosopher's stone which is to turn everything into gold, and to redeem man from the original sentence of his Maker, *in the sweat of his brow shall he eat his bread.* Not Quixote enough, however, to attempt to reason Bedlam to rights, my anxieties are turned to the most practicable means of withdrawing us from the ruin into which we have run.

Two hundred millions of paper in the hands of the people, (and less cannot be from the employment of a banking capital known to exceed one hundred millions,) is a fearful tax to fall at haphazard on their heads.

The debt which purchased our independence was but of eighty millions, of which twenty years of taxation had in 1809 paid but the one half. And what have we purchased with this tax of two hundred millions which we are to pay by wholesale but usury, swindling, and new forms of demoralization.

Revolutionary history has warned us of the probable moment when this baseless trash is to receive its fiat. Whenever so much of the precious metals shall have returned into the circulation as that every one can get some in exchange for his produce, paper, as in the Revolutionary war, will experience at once an universal rejection. When public opinion changes, it is with the rapidity of thought. Confidence is already on the totter, and every one now handles this paper as if playing at Robin's alive. That in the present state of the circulation the banks should resume payments in specie, would require their vaults to be like the widow's curse. The thing to be aimed at is, that the excesses of their emissions should be withdrawn as gradually, but as speedily, too, as if practicable, without so much alarm as to bring on the crisis dreaded.

Some banks are said to be calling in their paper. But ought we to let this depend on their discretion? Is it not the duty of the legislature to endeavor to avert from their constituents such a catastrophe as the extinguishment of two hundred millions of paper in their hands? The difficulty is indeed great; and the greater, because the patient revolts against all medicine.

I am far from presuming to say that any plan can be relied on with certainty, because the bubble may burst from one moment to another, but if it fails, we shall be but where we should have been without any effort to save ourselves.

[Letter to Colonel Charles Yancey, Monticello January 6, 1816]

EDUCATION

I think by far the most important bill in our whole code, is that for the diffusion of knowledge among the people. No other sure foundation can be devised, for the preservation of freedom and happiness. If anybody thinks that kings, nobles, or priests are good conservators of the public happiness, send him here [France]. It is the best school in the universe to cure him of that folly. He will see here, with his own eyes, that these descriptions of men are an abandoned confederacy against the happiness of the mass of the people.

Preach, my dear Sir, a crusade against ignorance; establish and improve the law for educating the common people. Let our countrymen know, that the people alone can protect us against these evils, and that the tax which will be paid for this purpose, is not more than the thousandth part of what will be paid to kings, priests and nobles, who will rise up among us if we leave the people in ignorance.

[Letter to Mr. Wythe. Paris, August 13, 1786]

By that part of our plan which prescribes the selection of youths of genius from among the classes of the poor, we hope to avail the State of those talents which nature has sown as liberally among the poor as the rich, but which perish without use, if not sought for and cultivated. But of the views of this law none is more important, none more legitimate, than that of rendering the people the safe, as they are the ultimate, guardians of their own liberty. For this purpose the reading in the first stage, where they will receive their whole education, is proposed, as has been said, to be chiefly historical. History, by apprizing them of the past, will enable them to judge of the future; it will avail them of the experience of other times and other nations; it will qualify them as judges of the actions and designs of men; it will enable them to know ambition under every disguise it may assume; and knowing it, to defeat its views. In every government on earth is some trace of human weakness, some germ of corruption and degeneracy, which cunning will discover, and wickedness insensibly open, cultivate and improve. Every government degenerates when trust to the rulers of the people alone. The people themselves therefore are its only safe depositories. And to render even them safe, their minds must be improved to a certain degree.

[**Notes on Virginia**]

I would have you determine beforehand to make yourself a thorough lawyer, and not be contented with a mere smattering. It is superiority of knowledge which can alone lift you above the heads of your competitors, and ensure your success. I think therefore you must calculate on devoting between two and three years to this course of reading, before you think of commencing practice. Whenever that begins, there is an end of reading.

[**Letter to John Garland Jefferson. New York, June 11, 1790**]

I do most anxiously wish to see the highest degrees of education given to the higher degrees of genius, and to all degrees of it, so much as may enable them to read and understand what is going on in the world, and to keep their part of it going on right: for nothing can keep it right but their own vigilant and distrustful superintendence. I do not believe with the Rochefoucaulds and Montaignes, that fourteen out of fifteen men are rogues: I believe a great abatement from that proportion may be made in favor of general honesty. But I have always found that rogues would be uppermost, and I do not know that the proportion is too strong for the higher orders, and for those who, rising above the swinish multitude, always contrive to nestle themselves into the places of power and profit. These rogues set out with stealing the people's good opinion, and then steal from them the right of withdrawing it, but contriving laws and associations against the power of the people themselves.

[**Letter to Mann Page.<@151>Monticello, August 30, 1795**]

I always hear with pleasure of institutions for the promotion of knowledge among my countrymen. The people of every country are the only safe guardians of their own rights, and are the only instruments which can be used for their destruction. And certainly they would never consent to be so used were they not deceived. To avoid this, they should be instructed to a certain degree. I have often thought that nothing would do more extensive good at small expense than the establishment of a small circulating library in every county, to consist of a few well-chosen books, to be lent to the people of the country, under such regulations as would secure their safe return in due time. These should be such as would give them a general view of other history, and particular view of that of their own country, a tolerable knowledge of Geography, the elements of Natural Philosophy, of Agriculture and Mechanics.

[Letter to John Wyche. Monticello, May 19, 1809]

EXAMPLE OF FREEDOM TO THE WORLD

We can surely boast of having set the world a beautiful example of a government reformed by reason alone, without bloodshed. But the world is too far oppressed, to profit by the example. On this side of the Atlantic, the blood of the people is become an inheritance, and those who fatten on it, will not relinquish it easily.

[Letter to E. Rutledge. Paris, July 18, 1788]

Though celebrated writers of this and other countries had already sketched good principles on the subject of government, yet the American war seems first to have awakened the thinking part of this nation in general from the sleep of despotism in which they were sunk. The officers too who had been to America, were mostly young men, less shackled by habit and prejudice, and more ready to assent to the dictates of common sense and common right. They came back impressed with these. The press, not withstanding its shackles, began to disseminate them; conversation, too, assume new freedom; politics became the theme of all societies, male and female, and a very extensive and zealous party was formed, which may be called the Patriotic party, who, sensible of the abusive government under which they lived, longed for occasions of reforming it.

[Letter to Dr. Price. Paris, January 8, 1789]

The enlightened part of Europe have given us the greatest credit for inventing the instrument of security for the rights of the people [Bill of Rights], and have been not a little surprised to see us so soon give it up.

[Letter to Francis Hopkinson. Paris, March 13, 1789]

Convinced that the republican is the only form of government which is not eternally at open or secret war with the rights of mankind, my prayers and efforts shall be cordially distributed to the support of that we have so happily established. It is indeed an animating thought, that while we are securing the rights of ourselves and our posterity, we are pointing out the way to struggling nations, who wish like us to emerge from their tyrannies also. Heaven help their struggles, and lead them, as it has done us, triumphantly through them.

[Letter to Wm. Hunter, Esq., Mayor. Alexandria, March 11, 1790]

The appeal to the rights of man, which had been made in the United States, was taken up by France, first of the European nations. From her, the spirit has spread over those of the South. The tyrants of the North have allied indeed against it; but it is irresistible. Their opposition will only multiply its millions of human victims; their own satellites will catch it, and the condition of man through the civilized world, will be finally and greatly ameliorated. This is a wonder instance of great events from small causes. So inscrutable is the arrangement of causes and consequences in this world, that a two-penny duty of tear, unjustly imposed in a sequestered part of it, changes the condition of all its inhabitants.

[The Autobiography of Thomas Jefferson]

A just and solid republican government maintained here, will be a standing monument and example for the aim and imitation of the people of other countries; and I join with you in the hope and belief that they will see, from our example, that a free government is of all others the most energetic; that the inquiry which has been excited among the mass of mankind by our revolution and its consequences, will ameliorate the condition of man over a great portion of the globe.

[Letter to John Dickinson.<@151>Washington, March 6, 1801]

The last hope of human liberty in this world rests on us. We ought, for so dear a state, to sacrifice every attachment and every enmity. Leave the President free to choose his own coadjutors, to pursue his own measures, and support him and them, even if we think we are wise than they, honester than they are, or possessing more enlarged information of the state of things. If we move in mass, be it ever so circuitously, we shall attain our object; but if we break into squads, every one pursuing the path he thinks most direct, we become an easy conquest to those who can now barely hold us in check. I repeat again, that we ought not to schismatize on either men or measures. Principles alone can justify that. If we find our government in all its branches rushing headlong, like our predecessors, into the arms of monarchy, if we find them violating our dearest rights, the trial by jury, the freedom of the press, the freedom of opinion, civil or religious, or opening on our peace of mind or personal safety the sluices of terrorism, if we see them raising standing armies, when the absence of all other danger points to these as the sole objects on which they are to be employed, then indeed let us withdraw and call the nation to its tents. But while our functionaires are wise, and honest, and vigilant, let us move compactly under their guidance, and we have nothing to fear. Things may here and there go a little wrong. It is not in their power to prevent it. But all will be right in the end, though not perhaps by the shortest means.

[Letter to Colonel William Duane. Monticello, March 28, 1811]

Old Europe will have to lean on our shoulders, and to hobble along by our side, under the monkish trammels of priests and kings, as she can. What a colossus shall we be when the southern continent comes up to our mark! What a stand will it secure as a ralliance for the reason and freedom of the globe! I like the dreams of the future better than the history of the past—so good night! I will dream on, always fancying that Mrs. Adams and yourself are by my side marking the progress and the obliquity's of ages and countries.

[Letter to John Adams. Monticello, August 1, 1816]

Yet I will not believe our labors are lost. I shall not die without a hope that light and liberty are on steady advance. We have seen, indeed, once within the records of history, a complete eclipse of the human mind continuing for centuries. And this, too, by swarms of the same northern barbarians, conquering and taking possession of the countries and governments of the civilized world. Should this be again attempted, should the same northern hordes, allured again by the corn, wine, and oil of the south, be able again to settle their swarms in the countries of their growth, the art of printing alone, and the vast dissemination of books, will maintain the mind where it is, and raise the conquering ruffians to the level of the conquered, instead of degrading these to that of their conquerors. And even should the cloud of barbarism and despotism again obscure the science and liberties of Europe, this country remains to preserve and restore light and liberty to them. In short, the flames kindled on the 4th of July, 1776, have spread over too much of the globe to be extinguished by the feeble engines of despotism; on the contrary, they will consume these engines and all who work them.

[Letter to John Adams. Monticello, September 12, 1821]

EXERCISE

Give about two of them [hours], every day, to exercise; for health must not be sacrificed to learning. A strong body makes the mind strong. As to the species of exercise, I advise the gun. While this gives a moderate exercise to the body, it gives boldness, enterprise, and independence to the mind. Games played with the ball, and others of that nature, are too violent for the body, and stamp no character on the mind. Let your gun, therefore, be the constant companion of your walks. Never think of taking a book with you. The object of walking is to relax the mind. You should therefore not permit yourself even to think while you walk; but divert yourself by the objects surrounding you. Walking is the best possible exercise. Habituate yourself to walk very far. The Europeans value themselves on having subdued the horse to the uses of man; but I doubt whether we have not lost more than we have gained, by the use of this animal. No one has occasioned so much the degeneracy of the human body. An Indian goes on foot nearly as far in a day, for a long journey, as an enfeebled white does on his horse; and he will tire the best horses. There is no habit you will value so much as that of walking far without fatigue. I would advise you to take your exercise in the afternoon; not because it is the best time for exercise, for certainly it is not; but because it is the best time to spare from your studies; and habit will soon reconcile it to health, and render it nearly as useful as if you gave to that the more precious hours of the day. A little walk of half an hour, in the morning, when you first rise, is advisable also. It shakes off sleep, and produces other good effects in the animal economy. Rise at a fixed and an early hour, and go to bed at a fixed and early hour also. Sitting up late at night is injurious to the health, and not useful to the mind.

[Letter to Peter Carr. Paris, August 19, 1785]

FARMING

The principles on which I calculate the value of life, are entirely in favor of my present course. I return to farming with an ardor which I scarcely knew in my youth, and which has got the better entirely of my love of study.

[Letter to John Adams. Monticello, April 25, 1794]

FOREIGN AFFAIRS

I often doubt whether I should trouble Congress or my friends with the details of European politics. I know they do not excite that interest in America, of which it is impossible for one to divest himself here. I know, too, that it is a maxim with us, and I think it a wise one, not to entangle ourselves with the affairs of Europe. Still, I think, we should know them. The Turks have practiced the same maxim of not meddling in the complicated wrangles of this continent. But they have unwisely chosen to be ignorant of them also, and it is this total ignorance of Europe, its combinations and its movements, which exposes them to that annihilation possibly about taking place. While there are powers in Europe which fear our views, or have views on us, we should keep an eye on them, their connections and oppositions, that in a moment of need, we may avail ourselves of their weakness with respect to others as well as ourselves, and calculate their designs and movements, on all the circumstances under which they exist. Though I am persuaded, therefore, that these details are read by many with great indifference, yet I think it my duty to enter into them, and to run the risk of giving too much, rather than too little information.

[Letter to E. Carrington. Paris, December 21, 1781]

In the transaction of your foreign affairs, we have endeavored to cultivate the friendship of all nations, and especially of those with which we have the most important relations. We have done them justice on all occasions, favored where favor was lawful and cherished mutual interests and inter-course on fair and equal terms. We are firmly convinced, and we act on that conviction, that with nations as with individuals, our interests soundly calculated, will ever be found inseparable from our moral duties; and history bears witness to the fact, that a just nation is taken on its word, when recourse is had to armaments and wars to bridle others.

[Second Inaugural Address. March 4, 1805]

We are alarmed here with the apprehensions of war; and sincerely anxious it may be avoided; but not at the expense with of our faith or honor. It seems much the general opinion here, the latter has been too much wounded not to require reparation, and to seek it even in war, if that be necessary. As to myself, I love peace, and I am anxious that we should give the world still another useful lesson, by showing to them other modes of punishing injuries by war, which is as much a punishment to the punisher as to the sufferer. I love, therefore, [the] proposition of cutting off all com-munication with the nation which has conducted itself so atrociously. This, you will say, may bring on war. If it does, we will meet it like men; but it may not bring on war, and then the experiment will have been a happy one. I believe this war would be vastly more unanimously approved than any one we ever were engaged in; because the aggressions have been so wanton and bare-faced, and so unquestionably against our desire.

[Letter to Tench Coxe. Monticello, May 1, 1794]

This, however, we have no right to meddle with. It suffices for us, if the moral and physical condition of our own citizens qualifies them to select the able and good for the direction of their government, with a recurrence of elections at such short periods as will enable them to displace an unfaithful servant, before the mischief he mediates may be irremediable.

[**Letter to John Adams. Monticello, October 28, 1813**]

I hope no American patriot will ever lose sight of the essential policy of interdicting in the seas and territories of both Americas, the ferocious and sanguinary contests of Europe. I wish to see this coalition begun. I am earnest for an agreement with the maritime powers of Europe, assigning them the task of keeping down the piracies of their seas and the cannibalism's of the African coasts, and to us, the suppression of the same enormities within our seas; and for this purpose, I should rejoice to see the fleets of Brazil and the United States riding together as brethren of the same family, and pursuing the same object. And indeed it would be of happy augury to begin at once this concert of action here, on the invitation of either to the other government, while the way might be preparing for withdrawing our cruisers from Europe, and preventing naval collisions there which daily endanger our peace.

[**Letter to William Short. Monticello, August 4, 1820**]

The question presented by the letters you have sent me, is the most momentous which has ever been offered to my contemplation since that of Independence. That made us a nation, this sets our compass and points the course which we are to steer through the ocean of time opening on us. And never could we embark on it under circumstances more auspicious. Our first and fundamental maxim should be, never to entangle ourselves in the broils of Europe. Our second, never to suffer Europe to intermeddle with cis-Atlantic affairs. America, North and South, has a set of interests distinct from those of Europe, and peculiarly her own. She should therefore have a system of her own, separate and apart from that of Europe. While the last is laboring to become the domicile of despotism, our endeavors should surely be, to make our hemisphere that of freedom. One nation, most of all, could disturb us in this pursuit; she now offers to lead, aid, and accompany us in it. By acceding to her proposition, we detach her from the bands, bring her mighty weight into the scale of free government, and emancipate a continent at one stroke, which might otherwise linger long in doubt and difficulty. Great Britain is the nation which can do us the most harm of any one, or all on earth; and with her on our side we need not fear the whole world. With her then, we should most sedulously cherish a cordial friendship; and nothing would tend more to knit our affections than to be fighting once more, side by side, in the same cause. Not that I would purchase her amity at the price of taking part in her wars. But the war in which the present proposition might engage us, should that be its consequence, is not her war but ours. Its object is to introduce and establish the American system, of keeping out of our land all foreign powers, of never permitting those of Europe to intermeddle with the affairs of our nations. It is to maintain our own principle, not to depart from it. And if, to facilitate this, we can effect a division in the body of European powers, and draw over to our side its most powerful member, surely we should do it. But I am clearly of Mr. Canning's opinion, that it will prevent instead of provoking war. With Great Britain withdrawn from their scale and shifted into that of our two continents, all Europe combined would not undertake such a war. For how would they propose to get at either enemy without superior fleets? Nor is the occasion to be slighted which this proposition offers, of declaring our protest against the atrocious violations of the rights of nations, by the interference of any one in the internal affairs of another, so flagitiously begun by Bonaparte, and now continued by the equally lawless Alliance, calling itself Holy.

But we have first to ask ourselves a question. Do we wish to acquire to our own confederacy any one or more of the Spanish provinces? I candidly confess, that I have ever looked on Cuba as the most interesting addition which could ever be made to our system of States. The control which, with Florida Point, this island would give us over the Gulf of Mexico, and the countries and isthmus bordering on it, as well as all those whose waters flow into it, would fill up the measure of our political well-being. Yet, as I am sensible that this can never be obtained, even with her own consent, but by war; and its independence, which is our second interest, (and especially its independence of England,) can be secured without it, I have no hesitation in abandoning my first wish to future chances, and accepting its independence, with peace and the friendship of England, rather than its association, at the expense of war and her enmity. I could honestly, therefore, join in the declaration proposed, that we aim not at the acquisition of any of those possessions, that we will not stand in the way of any amicable arrangement between them and the Mother country; but that we will oppose, with all our means, the forcible interposition of any other power, as auxiliary, stipendiary, or under any other form or pretext, and most especially, their transfer to any power by conquest, cession, or acquisition in any other way. I should think it, therefore, advisable, that the Executive should encourage the British government to a continuance in the dispositions expressed in these letters, by an assurance of his concurrence with them as far as his authority goes; and that as it may lead to war, the declaration of which requires an act of Congress, the case shall be laid before them for consideration at their first meeting, and under the reasonable aspect in which it is seen by himself.

[Letter to President James Monroe. Monticello, October 24, 1823]

FREE ENTERPRISE

Agriculture, manufacture, commerce, and navigation, the four pillars of our prosperity, are the most thriving when left most free to individual enterprise.

[Inauguration Address March 4, 1801]

FREEDOM OF SPEECH

A declaration, that the federal government will never restrain the presses from printing anything they please, will not take away the liability of the printers for false facts printed.

[Letter to James Madison. Paris, July 31, 1788]

FUTURE

I carry with me the consolation of a firm persuasion that Heaven has in store for our beloved country long ages to come of prosperity and happiness.

[Eighth Annual Message. November 8, 1808]

GEORGE WASHINGTON

I think I knew General Washington intimately and thoroughly; and were I called on to delineate his character, it should be in terms like these.

His mind was great and powerful, without being of the very first order; his penetration strong, though not so acute as that of a Newton, Bacon, or Lock; and as far as he saw, no judgement was ever sounder. It was slow in operation, being little aided by invention or imagination, but sure in conclusion. Hence the common remark of his officers, of the advantage he derived from councils of war, where hearing all suggestions, he selected whatever was best; and certainly no general ever planned his battles more judiciously. But if deranged during the course of the action, if any member of his plan was dislocated by sudden circumstances, he was slow in readjustment. The consequence was, that he often failed in the field, and rarely against an enemy in station, as at Boston and York.

He was incapable of fear, meeting personal dangers with the calmest unconcern. Perhaps the strongest feature in his character was prudence, never acting until every circumstance, every consideration, was maturely weighed; refraining if he saw a doubt, but, when once decided, going through with his purpose, whatever obstacles opposed. His integrity was most pure, his justice the most inflexible I have ever known, no motives of interest or consanguinity, of friendship or hatred, being able to bias his decision. He was, indeed, in every sense of the words, a wise, a good, and a great man. His temperament was naturally irritable and high toned; but reflection and resolution had obtained a firm and habitual ascendancy over it. If ever, however, it broke its bonds, he was most tremendous in his wrath.

In his expenses he was honorable, but exact; liberal in contributions to whatever promised utility; but frowning and unyielding on all visionary projects, and all unworthy calls on his charity. His heart was not warm in its affections; but he exactly calculated every man's value, and gave him a solid esteem proportioned to it. His person, you know, was fine, his stature exactly what one would wish, his deportment easy, erect and noble; the best horseman of his age, and the most graceful figure that could be seen on horseback. Although in the circle of his friends, where he might be unreserved with safety, he took a free share in conversation, his colloquial talents were not above mediocrity, possessing neither copiousness of ideas, nor fluency of words.

In public, when called on for a sudden opinion, he was unready, short and embarrassed. Yet he wrote readily, rather diffusely, in an easy and correct style. This he had acquired by conversation with the world, for his education was merely reading, writing and common arithmetic, to which he added surveying at a later day. His time was employed in action chiefly, reading little, and that only in agriculture and English history. His correspondence became necessarily extensive, and, with journalizing his agricultural proceedings, occupied most of his leisure hours within doors.

On the whole, his character was, in its mass, perfect, in nothing bad, in few points indifferent; and it may truly be said, that never did nature and fortune combine more perfectly to make a man great, and to place him in the same constellation with whatever worthies have merited from man an everlasting remembrance. For his was the singular destiny and merit, of leading the armies of his country successfully through an arduous war, for the establishment of its independence; of conducting its councils through the birth of a government, new in its forms and principles, until it had settled down into a quiet and orderly train; and of scrupulously obeying the laws through the whole of his career, civil and military, of which the history of the world furnishes no other example.

I am satisfied the great body of republicans think of him as I do. We were, indeed, dissatisfied with him on his ratification of the British treaty. But this was short lived. We knew his honesty, the wiles with which he was encompassed, and that age had already begun to relax the firmness of his purposes; and I am convinced he is more deeply seated in the love and gratitude of the republicans, than in the Pharisaical homage of the federal monarchists. For he was no monarchist from preference of his judgement. The soundness of that gave him correct view of the rights of man, and his severe justice devoted him to them. He has often declared to me that he considered our new Constitution as an experiment on the practicability of republican government, and with what dose of liberty man could be trusted for his own good; that he was determine the experiment should have a fair trial, and would lose the last drop of his blood in support of it. And these declarations he repeated to me the oftener and more pointedly, because he knew my suspicions of Colonel Hamilton's views, and probably had heard from him the same declarations which I had, to wit, that the British constitution, with its unequal representation, corruption and other existing abuses, was the most perfect government which had ever been established on earth, and that a reformation of those abuses would make it an impracticable government.

I do believe that General Washington had not a firm confidence in the durability of our government. He was naturally distrustful of men, and inclined to gloomy apprehensions; and I was ever persuaded that a belief that we must at length end in something like a British constitution, had some weight in his adoption of the ceremonies of levees, birthdays, pompous meetings with Congress, and other forms of the same character, calculated to prepare us gradually for a change which he believed possible, and to let it come on with as little shock as might be to the public mind.

These are my opinions of General Washington, which I would vouch at the judgement seat of God, having been formed on an acquaintance of thirty years. I served with him in the Virginia legislature from 1769 to the Revolutionary war, and again, a short time in Congress, until he left us to take command of the army. During the war and after it we corresponded occasionally, and in the four years of my continuance in the office of Secretary of State, our intercourse was daily, confidential and cordial.

After I retired from that office, great and malignant pains were taken by our federal monarchists, and not entirely without effect, to make him view me as a theorist, holding French principles of government, which would lead infallibly to licentiousness and anarchy. And to this he listened the more easily, from my known disapprobation of the British treaty. I never saw him afterwards, or these malignant insinuations should have been dissipated before his just judgement, as mists before the sun. I felt on his death, with my countrymen, that "verily a great man hath fallen this day in Israel."

[Letter to Dr. Walter Jones. January 2, 1814]

GOOD GOVERNMENT

That all should be satisfied with any one order of things is not to be expected, but I indulge the pleasing persuasion that the great body of our citizens will cordially concur in honest and disinterested efforts, which have for their object to preserve the general and State governments in their constitutional form and equilibrium; to maintain peace abroad, and and obedience to the laws at home; to establish principles and practices of administration favorable to the security of liberty and property, and to reduce expenses to what is necessary for the useful purposes of government.

[First Annual Message. December 8, 1801]

Expend the public money with the same care and economy we would practice with our own, and impose on our citizens no unnecessary burden; to keep in all things within the pale of our constitutional powers, and cherish the federal union as the only rock of safety these, fellow citizens, are the landmarks by which we are to guide ourselves in all our proceedings. By continuing to make these our rule of action, we shall endear to our countrymen the true principles of their constitution, and promote a union of sentiment and of actions equally auspicious to their happiness and safety.

[Second Annual Message. December 15, 1802]

But it is not by the consolidations, or concentration of powers, but by their distribution, that good government is effect. Were not this great country already divided into States, that division must be made, that each might do for itself what concerns itself directly, and what it can so much better do than a distant authority. Every State again is divided into counties, each to take care of what lies within its local bounds; each county again into townships or wards, to manage minuter details; and every ward into farms, to be governed each by its individual proprietor. Were we directed from Washington when to sow, and when to reap, we should soon want bread. It is by this partition of cares, descending in gradation from general to particular, that the mass of human affairs may be best managed, for the good and prosperity of all.

[The Autobiography of Thomas Jefferson]

The influence over government must be shared among all the people. If every individual which composes their mass participates of the ultimate authority, the government will be safe; because the corrupting the whole mass will exceed any private resources of wealth; and public ones cannot be provided but by levies on the people. In this case every man would have to pay his own price. The government of Great Britain has been corrupted, because but one man in ten has a right to vote for members of parliament. The sellers of the government, therefore, get nine-tenths of their price clear. It has been thought that corruption is restrained by confining the right of suffrage to a few of the wealthier of the people; but it would be more effectually restrained by an extension of that right to such members as would bid defiance to the means of corruption.

[Notes on Virgina]

I am for a government rigorously frugal and simple, applying all the possible savings of the public revenue to the discharge of the national debt; and not for a multiplication of officers and salaries merely to make partisans, and for increasing, by every device, the public debt, on the principle of its being a public blessing.

[Letter to Elbridge Gerry. Philadelphia, January 26, 1799]

The legitimate powers of government extend to such acts only as are injurious to others.

[Notes on Virginia]

Government is just as infallible, too, when it fixes systems in physics.

[Notes on Virginia]

I know, indeed, that some honest men fear that a republican government cannot be strong; that this government is not strong enough. But would the honest patriot, in the full tide of successful experiment, abandon a government which has so far kept us free and firm, on the theoretic and visionary fear that this government, the world's best hope, may by possibility want energy to preserve itself? I trust not. I believe this, on the contrary, the strongest government on earth. I believe it is the only one where every man, at the call of the laws, would fly to the standard of the law, and would meet invasions of the public order as his own personal concern.

Sometimes it is said that man cannot be trusted with the government of himself. Can he, then, be trusted with the government of others? Or have we found angels in the forms of kings to govern him? Let history answer this question.

Let us, then, with courage and confidence pursue our own federal and republican principles, our attachment to our union and representative government. Kindly separated by nature and a wide ocean from the exterminating havoc of one quarter of the globe; too high-minded to endure the degradations of the others; possessing a chosen country, with room enough for our descendants to the hundredth and thousandth generation; entertaining a due sense of our equal right to the use of our own faculties, to the acquisitions of our industry, to honor and confidence from our fellow citizens, resulting not from birth but from our actions and their sense of them; enlightened by a benign religion, professed, indeed, and practiced in various forms, yet all of them including honesty, truth, temperance, gratitude, and the love of man; acknowledging and adoring an overruling Providence, which by all its dispensations proves that it delights in the happiness of man here and his greater happiness hereafter; with all these blessings, what more is necessary to make us a happy and prosperous people? Still one thing more, fellow citizens<@151>a wise and frugal government, which shall restrain men from injuring one another, which shall leave them otherwise free to regulate their own pursuits of industry and improvement, and shall not take from the mouth of labor the bread it has earned. This is the sum of good government, and this is necessary to close the circle of our felicities.

[Inauguration Address. March 4, 1801]

Convinced that the republican is the only form of government which is not eternally at open or secret war with the rights of mankind, my prayers and efforts shall be cordially distributed to the support of that we have so happily established. It is indeed an animating thought, that while we are securing the rights of ourselves and our posterity, we are pointing out the way to struggling nations, who wish like us to emerge from their tyrannies also. Heaven help their struggles, and lead them, as it has done us, triumphantly through them.

[Letter to Wm. Hunter, Esq., Mayor of Alexandria. March 11, 1790]

We have chanced to live in an age which will probably be distinguished in history, for its experiments in government on a larger scale than has yet taken place. But we shall not live to see the result. The grosser absurdities, such as hereditary magistracies, we shall see exploded in our day, long experience having already pronounced condemnation against them. But what is to be the substitute? This our children or grandchildren will answer. We may be satisfied with the certain knowledge that none can ever be so tried, so stupid, so unrighteous, so oppressive, so destructive of every end for which honest men enter into government, as that which their forefathers had established, and their fathers alone venture to tumble headlong from the stations they have so long abused. It is unfortunate, that the efforts of mankind to recover the freedom of which they have been so long deprived, will be accompanied with violence, with errors, and even with crimes. But while we weep over the means, we must pray for the end.

Its inhabitants must be too much enlightened, too well experienced in the blessings of freedom and undisturbed industry, to tolerate long a contrary state of things. I should be happy to hear that their government perfects itself, and leaves room for the honest, the industrious and wise; in which case, your own talents, and those of the persons for whom you have interested yourself, will, I am sure, find welcome and distinction

[Letter to Monsieur D'Ivernois. Monticello, February 6, 1795]

No experiment can be more interesting than that we are now trying, and which we trust will end in establishing the fact, that man may be governed by reason and truth. Our first object should therefore be, to leave open to him all the avenues to truth. The most effectual hitherto found, is the freedom of the press. It is, therefore, the first shut up by those who fear the investigation of their actions. The firmness with which the people have withstood the late abuses of the press, the discernment they have manifested between truth and falsehood, show that they may safely be trusted to hear everything true and false, and to form a correct judgment between them. As little is it necessary to impose on their senses, or dazzle their minds by pomp, splendor, or forms. Instead of this artificial, how much surer is that real respect, which results from the use of their reason, and the habit of bringing everything to the test of common sense. I hold it, therefore, certain, that to open the doors of truth, and to fortify the habit of testing everything by reason, are the most effectual manacles we can rivet on the hands of our successors to prevent their manacling the people with their own consent. The panic into which they were artfully thrown in 1798, the frenzy which was excited in them by their enemies against their apparent readiness to abandon all the principles established for their own protection, seemed for awhile to countenance the opinions of those who say they cannot be trusted with their own government. But I never doubted their rallying; and they did rally much sooner than I expected.

On the whole, that experiment on their credulity has confirmed my confidence in their ultimate good sense and virtue.

[Letter to Judge John Tyler. Washington, June 28, 1804]

The only orthodox object of the institution of government is to secure the greatest degree of happiness possible to the general mass of those associated under it

[Letter to F.A. Van der Kemp. Monticello, March 22, 1812]

No, my friend, the way to have a good and safe government, is not to trust it all to one, but to divide it among the many, distributing to every one exactly the functions he is competent to. Let the national government be entrusted with the defense of the nation, and its foreign and federal relations; the State governments with the civil rights, laws, police, and administration of what concerns the State generally; the counties with the local concerns of the counties, and each ward direct the interests within itself. It is by dividing and subdividing these republics from the great national one down through all its subordination's, until it ends in the administration of every man's farm by himself; by placing under every one what his own eye may superintend, that all will be done for the best.

What has destroyed liberty and the rights of man in every government which has ever existed under the sun? The generalizing and concentrating all cares and powers into one body, no matter whether of the autocrats of Russian or France, or of the aristocrats of a Venetian senate. And I do believe that if the Almighty has not decreed that man shall never be free, (and it is a blasphemy to believe it,) that the secret will be found to be in the making himself the depository of the powers respecting himself, so far as he is competent to them, and delegating only what is beyond his competence by a synthetical process, to higher and higher orders of functionaries, so as to trust fewer and fewer powers in proportion as the trustees become more and more oligarchical. The elementary republics of the wards, the county republics, the State republics, and the republic of the Union, would form a gradation of authorities, standing each on the basis of law, holding every one its delegated share of powers, and constituting truly a system of fundamental balances and checks for the government. Where every man is a sharer in the direction of his ward-republic, or of some of the higher ones, and feels that he is a participator in the government of affairs, not merely at an election one day in the year, but every day; when there shall not be a man in the State who will not be a member of some one of its councils, great or small, he will let the heart be torn out of his body sooner than his power wrested from him by a Caesar or a Bonaparte.

How powerfully did we feel the energy of this organization in the case of embargo? I felt the foundations of the government shaken under my feet by the New England townships. There was not an individual in their States whose body was not thrown with all its momentum into action; and although the whole of the other States were known to be in favor of the measure, yet the organization of this little selfish minority enabled it to overrule the Union. What would the unwieldy counties of the Middle, the south, and the West do? Call a county meeting, and the drunken loungers at and about the courthouses would have collected, the distances being too great for the good people and the industrious generally to attend. The character of those who really met would have been the measure of the weight they would have had in the scale of public opinion. As Cato, then, concluded every speech with the words, "Carthago delenda est" so do I every opinion, with the injunction, "divide the counties into wards." Begin them only for a single purpose; they will soon show for what others they are the best instruments. God bless you, and all our rulers, and give them the wisdom, as I am sure they have the will, to fortify us against the degeneracy of our government, and the concentration of all its powers in the hands of the one, the few, the well-born or the many.

[Letter to Joseph C. Cabell. Monticello, February 2, 1816]

The equal rights of man, and the happiness of every individual, are now acknowledged to be the only legitimate objects of government. Modern times have the signal advantage, too, of having discovered the only device by which these rights can be secured, to wit: government by the people, acting not in person, but by representatives chosen by themselves, that is to say, by every man of ripe years and sane mind, who either contributes by his purse or person to the support of his country. Hereditary bodies, on the contrary, always existing, always on the watch for their own aggrandizement, profit of every opportunity of advancing the privileges of their order, and encroaching on the rights of the people.

[Letter to Monsieur A. Coray. Monticello, October 31, 1823]

But from Saratoga till we got back to Northhampton was then mostly desert. Now it is what thirty-four years of free and good government have made it. It shows how soon the labor of men would make a paradise of the whole earth, were it not for misgovernment, and a diversion of all his energies from their proper object "the happiness of man," to the selfish interests of kings, nobles, and priests.

[Letter to Ellen W. Coolidge. Monticello, August 27, 1825]

HAPPINESS

It is your future happiness which interests me, and nothing can contribute more to it (moral rectitude always excepted) than the contracting a habit of industry and activity. Of all the cankers of human happiness none corrodes with so silent, yet so baneful a tooth, as indolence. Body and mind both unemployed, our being becomes a burden, and every object about us loathsome, even the dearest. Idleness begets ennui, ennui the hypochondria, and that a diseased body. No laborious person was ever yet hysterical. Exercise and application produce order in our affairs, health of body, cheerfulness of mind, and these make us precious to our friends. You are not, however, to consider yourself an unemployed while taking exercise. That is necessary for your health, and health is the first of all objects.

[Letter to Martha Jefferson. Aix-en Provence, March 28, 1781]

If the public then has no claim on me, and my friends nothing to justify, the decision will rest on my own feelings alone. There has been a time when these were very different from what they are now; when perhaps the esteem of the world was of higher value in my eye than everything in it. But age, experience and reflection preserving to that only its due value, have set a higher on tranquillity. The motion of my blood no longer keeps time with the tumult of the world. It leads me to seek for happiness in the lap and love of my family, in the society of my neighbors and my books, in the wholesome occupations of my farm and my affairs, in an interest or affection in every bud that opens, in every breath that blows around me, in an entire freedom of rest, of motion of thought, owing account to myself alone of my hours and actions.

[Letter to James Madison. Philadelphia, June 9, 1793]

HEALTH

An attention to health then, should take place of every other object. The time necessary to secure this by active exercises, should be devoted to it, in preference to every other pursuit. I know the difficulty with which a studious man tears himself from his studies, at any given moment of the day. But his happiness, and that of his family, depend on it. The most uniformed mind, with a healthy body, is happier than the wisest valetudinarian.

[Letter to T. M. Randolph, Junior. Paris, July 6, 1787]

HOPE

There are, indeed, (who might say nay) gloomy and hypochondriac minds, inhabitants of diseased bodies, disgusted with the present, and despairing of the future; always counting that the worst will happen, because it may happen. To these I say, how much pain have cost us the evils which have never happened! My temperament is sanguine. I steer my bark with Hope in the head, leaving Fear astern. My hopes, indeed, sometimes fail; but not oftener than the forebodings of the gloomy.

[Letter to John Adams. Monticello, April 8, 1816]

INVENTIONS

It has been pretended by some, (and in England especially,) that inventors have a natural and exclusive right to their inventions, and not merely for their own lives, but inheritable to their heirs. But while it is a moot question whether the origin of any kind of property is derived from nature at all, it would be singular to admit and natural and even an hereditary right to inventors. It is agreed by those who have seriously considered the subject, that no individual has, of natural right, a separate property in an acre of land, for instance. By an universal law, indeed, whatever, whether fixed or movable, belongs to all men equally and in common, is the property for the moment of him who occupies it, but when he relinquishes the occupation, the property goes with it.

Stable ownership is the gift of social law, and is given late in the progress of society. It would be curious then, if an idea, the fugitive fermentation of an individual brain, could, of natural right, be claimed in exclusive and stable property. If nature has made any one thing less susceptible than all others of exclusive property, it is the action of the thinking power called an idea, which an individual may exclusively possess as long as he keeps it to himself; but the moment it is divulged, it forces itself into the possession of every one, and the receiver cannot dispossess himself of it. Its peculiar character, too, is that no one possess the less, because every other possesses the whole of it. He who receives an idea from me, receives instruction himself without lessening mine; as he who lights his taper at mine, receives light without darkening me.

That ideas should freely spread from one to another over the globe, for the moral and mutual instruction of man, and improvement of his condition, seems to have been peculiarly and benevolently designed by nature, when she made them, like fire, expansible over all space, without lessening their density in any point, and like the air in which we breathe, move, and have our physical being, incapable of confinement or exclusive appropriation.

Inventions then cannot, in nature, be a subject of property. Society may give an exclusive right to the profits arising from them, as an encouragement to men to pursue ideas which may produce utility, but this may or may not be done, according to the will and convenience of the society, without claim or complaint from anybody.

[Letter to Isaac McPherson. Monticello, August 13, 1813]

JOHN ADAMS

If Mr. Adams can be induced to administer the government on its true principles, and to relinquish his bias to an English constitution, it is to be considered whether it would not be on the whole for the public good to come to a good understanding with him as to his future elections. He is perhaps the only sure barrier against Hamilton's getting in.

[Letter to James Madison. Monticello, January 1, 1797]

You know the perfect coincidence of principle and of action, in the early part of the revolution, which produced a high degree of mutual respect and esteem between Mr. Adams and myself. Certainly no man was ever truer than he was, in that day, to those principles of rational republicanism which, after the necessity of throwing off our monarchy, dictated all our efforts in the establishment of a new government. And although he swerved, afterwards, towards the principles of the English constitution, our friendship did not abate on that account.

While he was Vice-President, and I Secretary of State, I received a letter from President Washington, then at Mount Vernon, desiring me to call together the Heads of departments, and to invite Mr. Adams to join us (which, by-the-bye, was the only instance of that being done) in order to determine of some measure which required dispatch; and he desired me to act on it, as decided, without again recurring to him. I invited them to dine with me, and after dinner, sitting at our wine, having settled our question, other conversation came on, in which a collision of opinion arose between Mr. Adams and Colonel Hamilton, on the merits of the British constitution, Mr. Adams giving it as his opinion, that, if some of its defects and abuses were corrected, it would be the most perfect constitution of government ever devised by man. Hamilton, on the contrary, asserted, that with its existing vices, it was the most perfect model of government that could be formed; and that the correction of its vices would render it an impracticable government. And this you may be assured was the real line of difference between the political principles of these two gentlemen.

Another incident took place on the same occasion, which will further delineate Mr. Hamilton's political principles. The room being hung around with a collection of the portraits of remarkable men, among them were those of Bacon, Newton, and Locke, Hamilton asked me who they were. I told him they were my trinity of the three greatest men the world had ever produced, naming them. He paused for some time: "the greatest man" said he, "that ever lived, was Julius Caesar" Mr. Adams was honest as a politician, as well as a man; Hamilton honest as a man, but, as a politician, believing in the necessity of either force or corruption to govern men.

You remember the machinery which the federalists played off, about that time, to beat down the friends to the real principles of our Constitution, to silence by terror every expression in their favor, to bring us into war with France and alliance with England, and finally to homologize our Constitution with that of England. Mr. Adams, you know, was overwhelmed with feverish addresses, dictated by the fear, and often by the pen, of the "bloody buoy", and was seduced by them into some open indications of his new principles of government, and in fact, was so elated as to mix with his kindness a little superciliousness towards me. Even Mrs. Adams, with all her good sense and prudence, was sensibly flushed. And you recollect the short suspension of our intercourse, and the circumstance which gave rise to it, which you were so good as to bring to an early explanation, and have set to rights, to the cordial satisfaction of us all.

The nation at length passed condemnation on the political principles of the federalists, by refusing to continue Mr. Adams in the Presidency. On the day on which we learned in Philadelphia the vote of the city of New York, which it was well known would decided the vote of the State, and that, again, the vote of the Union, I called on Mr. Adams on some official business. He was very sensibly affected, and accosted me with these words: "Well, I understand that you are to beat me in this contest, and I will only say that I will be as faithful a subject as any you will have."> "Mr. Adams," said I, "this is no personal contest between you and me. Two systems of principles on the subject of government divide our fellow citizens into two parties. With one of these you concur, and I with the other. As we have been longer on the public stage than most of those now living, our names happen to be more generally known. One of these parties, therefore, has put your name at its head, the other mine. Were we both to die to-day, to-morrow two other names would be in the place of ours, without any change in the motion of the machinery. Its motion is from its principle, not from you or myself." "I believe you are right," said he, "that we are but passive instruments, and should not suffer this matter to affect our personal dispositions." But he did not long retain this just view of the subject.

I have always believed that the thousand calumnies which the federalists, in bitterness of heart, and mortification at their ejection, daily invented against me, were carried to him by their busy intriguers, and made some impression. When the election between Burr and myself was kept in suspense by the federalists, and they were mediating to place the President of the Senate at the head of the government, I called on Mr. Adams with a view to have this desperate measure prevented by his negative. He grew warm in an instance, and said with a vehemence he had not used towards me before, "Sir, the event of the election is within your own power. You have only to say you will do justice to the public creditors, maintain the navy, and not disturb those holding offices, and the government will instantly be put into your hands. We know it is the wish of the people it should be so."

"Mr. Adams," said I, "I know not what part of my conduct, in either public or private life, can have authorized a doubt of my fidelity to the public engagements. I say, however, I will not come into the government by capitulation. I will not enter on it, but in perfect freedom to follow the dictates of my own judgment."

I had before given the same answer to the same intimation from Governor Morris. "Then," said he, "things must take their course."

I turned the conversation to something else, and soon took my leave. It was the first time in our lives we had ever parted with anything like dissatisfaction. And then followed those scenes of midnight appointment, which have been condemned by all men. The last day of his political power, the last hours, and even beyond the midnight, were employed in filling all offices, and especially permanent ones, with the bitterest federalists, and providing for me the alternative, either to execute the government by my enemies, whose study it would be to thwart and defeat all my measures, or to incur the odium of such numerous removals from office, as might bear me down.

A little time and reflection effaced in my mind this temporary dissatisfaction with Mr. Adams, and restored me to that just estimate of his virtues and passions, which a long acquaintance had enabled me to fix. And my first wish became that of making his retirement easy by any means in my power; for it was understood he was not rich. I suggested to some republican members of the delegation from his State, the giving him, either directly or indirectly, an office, the most lucrative in that State, and then offered to be resigned, if they thought he would not deem it affrontive. They were of opinion he would take great offence at the offer; and moreover, that the body of republicans would consider such a step in the outset as auguring very ill of the course I meant to pursue. I dropped the idea, therefore, but did not cease to wish for some opportunity of renewing our friendly understanding.

Two or three years after, having had the misfortune to lose a daughter, between whom and Mrs. Adams there had been a considerable attachment, she made it the occasion of writing me a letter, in which, with the tenderest expressions of concern at this event, she carefully avoided a single one of friendship towards myself, and even concluded it with the wishes "of her who 'once' took pleasure in subscribing herself your friend, Abigail Adams."

Unpromising as was the complexion of this letter, I determined to make an effort towards removing the cloud from between us. This brought on a correspondence which I now enclose for your perusal, after which be so good as to return it to me, as I have never communicated it to any mortal breathing, before. I send it to you, to convince you I have not been wanting either in the desire, or the endeavor to remove his misunderstanding. Indeed, I thought it highly disgraceful to us both, as indicating minds not sufficiently elevated to prevent a public competition from affecting our personal friendship. I soon found from the correspondence that conciliation was desperated, and yielding to an intimation in her last letter, I ceased from further explanation.

I have the same good opinion of Mr. Adams which I ever had. I know him to be an honest man, an able one with his pen, and he was a powerful advocate on the floor of Congress. He has been alienated from me, by belief in the lying suggestions contrived for electioneering purposes, that I perhaps mixed in the activity and intrigues of the occasion. My most intimate friends can testify that I was perfectly passive. They would sometimes, indeed, tell me what was going on; but no man ever heard me take part in such conversations; and none ever misrepresented Mr. Adams in my presence, without my asserting his just character. With very confidential persons I have doubtless disapproved of the principles and practices of his administration. This was unavoidable. But never with those with whom it could do him any injury. Decency would have required this conduct from me, if disposition had not; and I am satisfied Mr. Adams' conduct was equally honorable towards me. But I think it part of his character to suspect foul play in those of whom he is jealous, and not easily to relinquish his suspicions.

[Letter to Dr. Benjamin Rush. Monticello, January 16, 1811]

JUDGES

In the arguments in favor of a declaration of rights, you omit one which has great weight with me; the legal check which it puts into the hands of the judiciary. This is a body, which, if rendered independent and kept strictly to their own department, merits great confidence for their learning and integrity.

[Letter to James Madison. Paris, March 15, 1789]

It is not enough that honest men are appointed Judges. All know the influence of interest of the mind of man, and how unconsciously his judgment is warped by that influence. To this bias add that of the "espirit de corps", of their peculiar maxim and creed, that "it is the office of a good Judge to enlarge his jurisdiction," and the absence of responsibility; and how can we expect impartial decision between the General government, of which they are themselves so eminent a part, and an individual State, from which they have nothing to hope or fear? We have seen, too, that contrary to all correct example, they are in the habit of going out of the question before them, to throw an anchor ahead, and grapple further hold for future advances of power. They are then, in fact, the corps of sappers and miners, steadily working to undermine the independent rights of the States, and to consolidate all power in the hands of that government in which they have so important a freehold estate. But it is not by the consolidation, or concentration of powers, but by their distribution that good government is effected.

[Autobiography of Thomas Jefferson. January 6, 1821]

In truth, it is better to toss up cross and pile in a cause, than to refer it to a judge whose mind is warped by any motive whatever, in that particular case. But the common sense of twelve honest men gives still a better chance of just decision, than the hazard of cross and pile.

[Notes on Virginia]

LAWS

The instability of our laws is really an immense evil. I think it would be well to provide in our constitutions, that there shall always be a twelve month between the engrossing a bill and passing it; that it should then be offered to its passage without changing a word; and that if circumstances should be thought to require a speedier passage, it should take two-thirds of both Houses, instead of a bare majority.

[Letter to James Madison. Paris, December 20, 1781]

A strict observance of the written laws is doubtless "one" of the high duties of a good citizen, but it is not the "highest". The laws of necessity, of self-preservation, of saving our country when in danger, are of higher obligation. To lose our country by a scrupulous adherence to written law, would be to lose the law itself, with life, liberty, property and all those who are enjoying them with us; thus absurdly sacrificing the end to the means. When, in the battle of Germantown, General Washington's army was annoyed from Chew's house, he did not hesitate to plant his cannon against it, although the property of a citizen. When he besieged Yorktown, he leveled the suburbs, feeling that the laws of property must be postponed to the safety of the nation. While the army was before York, the Governor of Virginia took horses, carriages, provisions and even men by force, to enable that army to stay together till it could master the public enemy; and he was justified. A ship at sea in distress for provisions, meets another having abundance, yet refusing a supply; the law of self-preservation authorizes the distressed to take a supply by force. In all these cases, the unwritten laws of necessity, of self-preservation, and of the public safety, control the written laws of "meum" and "tuum".

[Letter to J. B. Colvin. Monticello, September 20, 1810]

LIMITED GOVERNMENT

I am convinced that those societies (as the Indians) which live without government, enjoy in their general mass an infinitely greater degree of happiness than those who live under the European governments. Among the former, public opinion is in the place of law, and restrains morals as powerfully as laws ever did anywhere. Among the latter, under pretence of governing, they have divided their nations into two classes, wolves and sheep. I do not exaggerate. This is a true picture of Europe. Cherish, therefore, the spirit of our people, and keep alive their attention. Do not be too severe upon their errors, but reclaim them by enlightening them. If once they become inattentive to the public affairs, you and I, and Congress and Assemblies, Judges and Governors, shall all become wolves.

[Letter to Colonel Edward Carrington. Paris, January 16, 1787]

The natural progress of things is for liberty to yield and government to gain ground. As yet our spirits are free. Our jealousy is only put to sleep by the unlimited confidence we all repose in the person to whom we all look as our president [Washington]. After him inferior characters may perhaps succeed, and awaken us to the danger which his merit has led us into.

[Letter to Colonel Carrington. Paris, May 27, 1788]

Agriculture, manufacture, commerce, and navigation, the four pillars of our prosperity, are the most thriving when left most free to individual enterprise.

[**Inauguration Address. March 4, 1801**]

The legitimate powers of government extend to such acts only as are injurious to others.

[**Notes on Virgina**]

THE LOUISIANA PURCHASE

To the Senate and House of Representatives of the United States:

In calling you together, fellow citizens, at an earlier day than was contemplated by the act of the last session of Congress, I have not been insensible to the personal inconveniences necessarily resulting from an unexpected change in your arrangements. But matters of great public concernment have rendered this call necessary, and the interest you feel in these will supersede in your minds all private considerations.

Congress witnessed, at their last session, the extraordinary agitation produced in the public mind by the suspension of our right of deposit at the port of New Orleans, no assignment of another place having been made according to treaty. They were sensible that the continuance of the privation would be more injurious to our nation than any consequences which could flow from any mode of redress, but reposing just confidence in the good faith of the government whose officer had committed the wrong, friendly and reasonable representations were resorted to, and the right of deposit was restored.

Previous, however, to this period, we had not been unaware of the danger to which our peace would be perpetually exposed while so important a key to the commerce of the western county remained under foreign power.

Difficulties, too, were presenting themselves as to the navigation of other streams, which, arising within our territories, pass through those adjacent. Propositions had, therefore, been authorized for obtaining, on fair conditions, the sovereignty of New Orleans, and of other possessions in that quarter interesting to our quiet, to such extent as was deemed practicable; and the provisional appropriation of two millions of dollars, to be applied and accounted for by the president of the United States, intended as part of the price, was considered as conveying the sanction of Congress to the acquisition proposed.

The enlightened Government of France saw, with just discernment, the importance to both nations of such liberal arrangements as might best and permanently promote the peace, friendship, and interests of both; and the property and sovereignty of all Louisiana, which had been restored to them, have on certain conditions been transferred to the United States by instruments bearing date the 30th of April last. When these shall have received the constitutional sanction of the senate, they will without delay be communicated to the representatives also, for the exercise of their functions, as to those conditions which are within the powers vested by the constitution in Congress.

While the property and sovereignty of the Mississippi and its waters secure an independent outlet for the produce of the western States, and an uncontrolled navigation through their whole course, free from collision with other powers and the dangers to our peace from that source, the fertility of the country, its climate and extent, promise in due season important aids to our treasury, an ample provision for our posterity, and a wise-spread field for the blessings of freedom and equal laws.

With the wisdom of Congress it will rest to take those ulterior measures which may be necessary for the immediate occupation and temporary government of the country; for its incorporation into our Union; for rendering the change of government a blessing to our newly-adopted brethren; for securing to them the rights of

conscience and of property; for confirming to the Indian inhabitants their occupancy and self-government, establishing friendly and commercial relations with them, and for ascertaining the geography of the country acquired. Such material for your information, relative to its affairs in general, as the short space of time has permitted me to collect, will be laid before you when the subject shall be in a state for your consideration.

With many other Indian tribes, improvements in agriculture and household manufacture are advancing, and with all our peace and friendship are established on grounds much firmer than heretofore. The measure adopted of establishing trading houses among them, and of furnishing them necessaries in exchange for their commodities, at such moderated prices as leave no gain, but cover us from loss, has the most conciliatory and useful effect upon them, and is that which will best secure their peace and good will.

Should the acquisition of Louisiana be constitutionally confirmed and carried into effect, a sum of nearly thirteen millions of dollars will then be added to our public debt, most of which is payable after fifteen years; before which term the present existing debts will all be discharged by the established operation of the sinking fund. When we contemplate the ordinary annual augmentation of imposts from increasing population and wealth, the augmentation of the same revenue by its extension to the new acquisition, and the economies which may still be introduced into our public expenditures, I cannot but hope that Congress in reviewing their resources will find means to meet the intermediate interests of this additional debt without recurring to new taxes, and applying to this object only the ordinary progression of our revenue. Its extraordinary increase in times of foreign war will be the proper and sufficient fund for any measures of safety or precaution which that state of things may render necessary in our neutral position.

[**Third Annual Message. October 17, 1803**]

I have said, fellow citizens, that the income reserved had enabled us to extend our limits; but that extension may possibly pay for itself before we are called on, and in the meantime, may keep down the accruing interest; in all events, it will repay the advances we have made. I know that the acquisition of Louisiana has been disapproved by some, from a candid apprehension that the enlargement of our territory would endanger its union. But who can limit the extent to which the federative principle may operate effectively? The larger our association, the less it will be shaken by local passions; and in any view, is it not better that the opposite bank of the Mississippi should be settled by our own brethren and children, than by strangers of another family? With which shall we be most likely to live in harmony and friendly intercourse?

[**Second Inaugural Address. March 4, 1805**]

I accept with pleasure, and with pleasure reciprocate your congratulations on the acquisition of Louisiana; for it is a subject of mutual congratulation, as it interests every man of the nation. The territory acquired, as it includes all the waters of the Missouri and Mississippi, has more than doubled the area of the United States, and the new parts is not inferior to the old in soil, climate, productions and important communications. If our Legislature dispose of it with the wisdom we have a right to expect, they may make it the means of tempting all our Indians on the east side of the Mississippi to remove to the west, and of condensing instead of scattering our population.

[Letter to General Horatio Gates. Washington, July 11, 1803]

MAJORITY RULE

The abandoning the principle of necessary rotation in the Senate, has, I see, been disapproved by many; in the case of the President, by none. I readily, therefore, suppose my opinion wrong, when opposed by the majority, as in the former instance, and the totality, as in the latter. In this, however, I should have done it with more complete satisfaction, had we all judged from the same position. To inculcate on minorities the duty of acquiescence in the will of the majority; and on majorities a respect for the rights of the minority.

[Letter to William Bache. Philadelphia, February 2, 1800]

All, too, will bear in mind this sacred principle, that though the will of the majority is in all cases to prevail, that will, to be rightful, must be reasonable; that the minority possess their equal rights, which equal laws must protect, and to violate which would be oppression.

[Inauguration Address. March 4, 1801]

The majority, then, has a right to depute representatives to a convention, and to make the Constitution what they think will be the best for themselves. But how collect their voice? This is the real difficulty. If invited by private authority, or county or district meetings, these divisions are so large that few will attend; and their voice will be imperfectly, or falsely, pronounced. Here, then, would be one of the advantages of the ward divisions I have proposed. The major of every ward, on a question like the present, would call his ward together, take the simple yea or nay of its members, convey these to the county court, who would hand on those of all its wards to be the proper general authority; and the voice of the whole people would be thus fairly, fully, and peaceably expressed, discussed, and decided by the common reason of the society. If this avenue be shut to the call of sufferance, it will make itself heard through that of force, and we shall go on as other nations are doing, in the endless circle of oppression, rebellion, reformation; and oppression, rebellion, reformation, again; and so on forever.

[Letter to Samuel Kercheval. Monticello, July 12, 1816]

The first principle of republicanism is, that the "lex majoris partis" is the fundamental law of every society of individuals of equal rights; to consider the will of the society enounced by the majority of a single vote, as sacred as if unanimous, is the first of all lessons in importance, yet the last which is thoroughly learnt. This law once disregarded, no other remains but that of force, which ends necessarily in military depotism.

[Letter to Baron Alexander von Humboldt. Monticello, June 13, 1817]

THE MEDIA

During this course of administration, and in order to disturb it, the artillery of the press has been leveled against us, charged with whatsoever its licentiousness could devise or dare. These abuses of an institution so important to freedom and science, are deeply to be regretted, inasmuch as they tend to lessen its usefulness, and to sap its safety; they might, indeed, have been corrected by the wholesome punishments reserved and provided by the laws of the several States against falsehood and defamation; but public duties more urgent press on the time of public servants, and the offenders have therefore been left to find their punishment in the public indignation.

No inference is here intended, that the laws provided by the State against false and defamatory publications, should not be enforced; he who has time, renders a service to public morals and public tranquillity, in reforming these abuses by the salutary coercion's of the law; but the experiment is noted, to prove that, since truth and reason have maintained their ground against false opinions in league with false facts, the press, confined to truth, needs no other legal restraint; the public judgement will correct false reasonings and opinions, on a full hearing of all parties; and no other definite line can be drawn between the inestimable liberty of the press and its demoralizing licentiousness. If there be still improprieties which this rule would not restrain, its supplement must be sought in the censorship of public opinion.

[Second Inaugural Address. March 4, 1805]

I am persuaded myself that the good sense of the people will always be found to be the best army. They may be led astray for a moment, but will soon correct themselves. The people are the only censors of their governors; and even their errors will tend to keep these to the true principles of their institution. To punish these errors too severely would be to suppress the only safeguard of the public liberty. The way to prevent these irregular interposition's of the people, is to give them full information of their affairs through the channel of the public papers, and to contrive that those papers should penetrate the whole mass of the people. The basis of our governments being the opinion of the people, the very first object should be to keep that right; and were it left to me to decided whether we should have a government without newspapers, or newspapers without a government, I should not hesitate a moment to prefer the latter. But I should mean that every man should receive those papers, and be capable of reading them.

[Letter to Colonel Edward Carrington. Paris, January 16, 1781]

To your request of my opinion of the manner in which a newspaper should be conducted, so as to be most useful, I should answer, "by restraining it to true facts and sound principles only." Yet I fear such a paper would find few subscribers. It is a melancholy truth, that a suppression of the press could not more completely deprive the nation of its benefits, than is done by its abandoned prostitution to falsehood. Nothing can now be believed which is seen in a newspaper. Truth itself becomes suspicious by being put into that polluted vehicle. The real extent of this state of misinformation is known only to those who are in situations to confront facts within their knowledge with the lies of the day.

I really look with commiseration over the great body of my fellow citizens, who, reading newspapers, live and die in the belief, that they have known something of what has been passing in the world in their time; whereas the accounts they have read in newspapers are just as true a history of any other period of the world as of the present, except that the real names of the day are affixed to their fables.

General facts may indeed be collected from them, such as that Europe is now at war, that Bonaparte has been a successful warrior, that he has subjected a great portion of Europe to his will, etc., etc.; but no details can be relied on. I will add, that the man who never looks into a newspaper is better informed than he who reads them; inasmuch as he who knows nothing is nearer to the truth than he whose mind is filled with falsehoods and errors. He who reads nothing will still learn the great facts, and the details are all false.

Perhaps an editor might begin a reformation in some such way as this. Divide his paper into four chapters, heading the 1st, Truths. 2d, Probabilities. 3d, Possibilities. 4th, Lies. The first chapter would be very short, as it would contain little more than authentic papers, and information from such sources, as the editor would be willing to risk his own reputation for their truth. The second would contain what, from a mature consideration of all circumstances, his judgment should conclude to be probably true. This, however, should rather contain too little than too much. The third and fourth should be professedly for those readers who would rather have lies for their money than the blank paper they would occupy. Such an editor too, would have to set his face against the demoralizing practice of feeding the public mind habitually on slander, and the depravity of taste which this nauseous aliment induce.

Defamation is becoming a necessary of life; insomuch, that a dish of tea in the morning or evening cannot be digested without this stimulant. Even those who do not believe these abominations, still read them with complaisance to their auditors, and instead of the abhorrence and indignation which should fill a virtuous mind, betray a secret pleasure in the possibility that some may believe them, though they do not themselves. It seems to escape them, that it is not he who prints, but he who pays for printing a slander, who is its real author.

[**Letter to John Norvell. Washington, June 11, 1807**]

MEDICINE

Was the government to prescribe to us our medicine and diet, our bodies would be in such keeping as our souls are now. Thus in France the emetic was once forbidden as a medicine, the potato as an article of food.

[Notes on Virginia]

MORALS

Give up money, give up fame, give up science, give up the earth itself and all it contains, rather than do an immoral act. And never suppose, that in any possible situation, or under any circumstances, it is best for you to do a dishonorable thing, however slightly so it may appear to you. Whenever you are to do a thing, though it can never be known but to yourself, ask yourself how you would act were all the world looking at you, and act accordingly. Encourage all your virtuous dispositions, and exercise them whenever an opportunity arises; being assured that they will gain strength by exercise, as a limb of the body does, and that exercise will make them habitual.

From the practice of the purest virtue, you may be assured you will derive the most sublime comforts in every moment of life, and in the moment of death. If ever you find yourself environed with difficulties and perplexing circumstances, out of which you are at a loss how to extricate yourself, do what is right, and be assured that that will extricate you the best out of the worst situations. Though you cannot see, when you take one step, what will be the next, yet follow truth, justice, and plain dealing, and never fear their leading you out of the labyrinth, in the easiest manner possible. The knot which you thought a Gordian one, will untie itself before you.

Nothing is so mistaken as the supposition, that a person is to extricate himself from a difficulty, by intrigue, by chicanery, by dissimulation, by trimming, by an untruth, an injustice. This increase the difficulties tenfold; and those who pursue these methods, get themselves so involved at length, that they can turn no way but their infamy becomes more exposed. It is of great importance to set a resolution, not to be shaken, never to tell an untruth. There is no vice so mean, so pitiful, so contemptible; and he who permits himself to tell a lie once, finds it much easier to do it a second and third time, till at length it becomes habitual; he tells lies without attending to it, and truths without the world's believing him. This falsehood of the tongue leads to that of the heart, and in time depraves all its good dispositions.

[Letter to Peter Carr. Paris, August 19, 1785]

Moral Philosophy. I think it lost time to attend lectures on this branch. He who made us would have been a pitiful bungler, if he had made the rules of our moral conduct a matter of science. For one man of science, there are thousands who are not. What would have become of them? Man was destined for society. His morality, therefore, was to be formed to this object. He was endowed with a sense of right and wrong, merely relative to this. This sense is as much a part of his nature, as the sense of hearing, seeing, feeling; it is the true foundation of morality, and not the "The Beautiful", truth, &c., as fanciful writers have imagined.

The moral sense, or conscience, is as much a part of man as his leg or arm. It is given to all human beings in a stronger or weaker degree, as force of members is given them in a greater or less degree. It may be strengthened by exercise, as may any particular limb of the body. This sense is submitted, indeed, in some degree, to the guidance of reason; but it is a small stock which is required for this: even a less one than what we call common sense.

State a moral case to a ploughman and a professor. The former will decide it as well, and often better than the latter, because he has not been led astray by artificial rules. In this branch, therefore, read good books, because they will encourage, as well as direct your feelings. The writings of Sterne, particularly, form the best course of morality that ever was written. Besides these, read the books mentioned in the enclosed paper; and, above all things, lose no occasion of exercising your dispositions to be grateful, to be generous, to be charitable, to be humane, to be true, just, firm, orderly, courageous, &c. Consider every act of this kind, as an exercise which will strengthen your moral faculties and increase your worth.

[Letter to Peter Carr. Paris, August 10, 1787]

THE NATIONAL DEBT

The conclusion then, is, that neither the representatives of a nation, nor the whole nation itself assembled, can validly engage debts beyond what they may pay in their won time, that is to say, within thirty-four years of the date of the engagement.

But with respect to future debts, would it not be wise and just for that nation to declare in the constitution they are forming, that neither the legislature nor the nation itself, can validly contract more debt than they may pay within their own age, or within the term of thirty-four years?

At first blush it may be laughed at, as the dream of a theorist; but examination will prove it to be solid and salutary. It would furnish matter for a fine preamble to our first law for appropriating the public revenue; and it will exclude, at the threshold of our new government, the ruinous and contagious errors of this quarter of the globe, which have armed despots with means which nature does not sanction, for binding in chains their fellow-men.

We have already given, in example, one effectual check to the dog of war, by transferring the power of declaring war from the executive to the legislative body, from those who are to spend, to those who are to pay. I should be pleased to see this second obstacle held out by us also, in the first instance. No nation can make a declaration against the validity of long-contracted debts, so disinterestedly as we, since we do not owe a shilling which will not be paid, principal and interest, by the measures you have taken, within the time of our own lives.

[**Letter to James Madison. Paris, September 6, 1789**]

Without encroaching on the rights of future generations, by burdening them with the debts of the past.

[**Second Inaugural Address. March 4, 1805**]

I am not among those who fear the people. They, and not the rich, are our dependence for continued freedom. And to preserve their independence, we must not let our rulers load us with perpetual debt. We must make our election between "economy and liberty", or "profusion and servitude".

If we run into such debts, as that we must be taxed in our meat and in our drink, in our necessaries and our comforts, in our labors and our amusements, for our callings and our creeds, as the people of England are, our people, like them, must come to labor sixteen hours in the twenty-four, give the earnings of fifteen of these to the government for their debts and daily expenses; and the sixteenth being insufficient to afford us bread, we must live, as they now do, on oatmeal and potatoes; have no time to think, no means of calling the mismanagers to account; but be glad to obtain subsistence by hiring ourselves to rivet their chains on the necks of our fellow suffers.

Our land-holders, too, like theirs, retaining indeed the title and steward-ship of estates called theirs, but held really in trust for the treasury, must wander, like theirs, in foreign countries, and be contented with penury, obscurity, exile, and the glory of the nation. This example reads to us the salutary lesson, that private fortunes are destroyed by public as well as by private extravagance. And this is the tendency of all human governments.

A departure in principle in one instance becomes a precedent for a second; that second for a third; and so on, till the bulk of society is reduced to mere automations of misery, to have no sensibilities left but for sinning and suffering. Then begins, indeed, the "bellum omnium in omnia", which some philosophers observing to be so general in this world, have mistaken it for the natural, instead of the abusive state of man. And the fore horse of this frightful team is public debt. Taxation follows that, and in its trains wretchedness and oppression.

[Letter to Samuel Kercheval. Monticello, July 12, 1816]

But with respect to future debts, would it not be wise and just for that nation to declare in the constitution they are forming, that neither the leg-islature nor the nation itself, can validly contract more debt than they may pay within their own age, or within the term of thirty-four years? And that all future contracts shall be deemed void, as to what shall remain unpaid at the end of thirty-four years from their date? This would put the lenders, and the borrowers also, on their guard. By reducing, too, the faculty of borrowing within its natural limits, it would bridle the spirit of war, to which too free a course has been procured by the inattention of money lenders to this law of nature, that succeeding generations are not responsible for the preceding.

[Letter to James Madison. Paris, September 6, 1789]

I am for a government rigorously frugal and simple, applying all the possible savings of the public revenue to the discharge of the national debt; and not for a multiplication of officers and salaries merely to make partisans, and for increasing, by every device, the public debt, on the principle of its being a public blessing.

[Letter to Elbridge Gerry. Philadelphia, January 26, 1799]

Funding I consider as limited, rightfully, to a redemption of the debt within the lives of a majority of the generation contracting it; every generation coming equally, by the laws of the Creator of the world to the free possession of the earth. He made for their subsistence, unencumbered by their predecessors, who, like them, were but tenants for life.

[Letter to John Taylor. Monticello, May 28, 1816]

NATIONAL DEFENSE

For a people who are free, and who mean to remain so, a well-organized and armed militia is their best security. It is, therefore, incumbent upon us, at every meeting, to revise the condition of the militia, and to ask ourselves if it is prepared to repel a powerful enemy at every point of our territories exposed to invasion.

[Eight Annual Message. November 8, 1808]

Weakness provokes insult and injury, while a condition to punish, often prevents them. This reasoning leads to the necessity of some naval force; that being the only weapon by which we can reach an enemy. I think it to our interest to punish the first insult; because an insult unpunished is the parent of many others.

[Letter to John Jay Paris, August 23, 1785]

I am for relying, for internal defense, on our militia solely, till actual invasion, and for such a naval force only as may protect our coasts and harbors from such depredations as we have experienced; and not for a standing army in time of peace, which may overawe the public sentiment; nor for a navy, which, by its expenses and the eternal wars in which it will implicate us, will grind us with public burdens, and sink us under them.

I am for free commerce with all nations; political connection with none; and little or no diplomatic establishment. And I am not for linking ourselves by new treaties with the quarrels of Europe; entering that field of slaughter to preserve their balance, or joining in the confederacy of kings to war against the principles of liberty.

[Letter to Elbridge Gerry. Philadelphia, January 26, 1799]

To this state of general peace with which we have been blessed, one only exception exists. Tripoli, the least considerable of the Barbary States, had come forward with demands unfounded either in right or in compact, and had permitted itself to denounce war, on our failure to comply before a given day. The style of the demand admitted but one answer. I set a small squadron of frigates into the Mediterranean, with assurances to that power of our sincere desire to remain in peace, but with orders to protect our commerce against the threatened attack. The measure was seasonable and salutary. The bey had already declared war in form. His cruisers were out. Two had arrived at Gibraltar. Our commerce in the Mediterranean was blockaded, and that of the Atlantic in peril. The arrival of our squadron dispelled the danger. One of the Tripolitan cruisers having fallen in with, and engaged the small schooner Enterprise, commanded by Lieutenant Sterret, which had gone as a tender to our larger vessels, was captured, after a heavy slaughter of her men, without the loss of a single one on our part. The bravery exhibited by our citizens on that element, will, I trust, be a testimony to the world that it is not the want of the virtue which makes us seek their peace, but a conscientious desire to direct the energies of our nation to the multiplication of the human race, and not to its destruction. Unauthorized by the constitution, without the sanction of Congress, to go beyond the line of defense, the vessel being disabled from committing further hostilities, was liberated with its crew. The legislature will doubtless consider whether, by authorizing measures of offence, also, they will place our force on an equal footing with that of its adversaries. I communicate all material information on this subject, that in the exercise of the important function confided by the constitution to the legislature exclusively, their judgment may form itself on a knowledge and consideration of every circumstance of weight.

[First Annual Message. December 8, 1801]

While noticing the irregularities committed on the ocean by others, those on our own part should not be omitted nor left unprovided for. Complaints have been received that persons residing within the United States have taken on themselves to arm merchant vessels, and to force a commerce into certain ports and countries in defiance of the laws of those countries. That individuals should undertake to wage private war, independently of the authority of their country, cannot be permitted in a well-ordered society. Its tendency to produce aggression on the laws and rights of other nations, and to endanger the peace of our own is so obvious, that I doubt not you will adopt measures for restraining it effectually in future.

[Fourth Annual Message. November 8, 1804]

NATIVE AMERICANS

Among our Indian neighbors, also, a spirit of peace and friendship generally prevails; and I am happy to inform you that the continued efforts to introduce among them the implements and the practice of husbandry, and of the household arts, have not been without success; that they are becoming more and more sensible of the superiority of this dependence for clothing and subsistence over the precarious resources of hunting and fishing; and already we are able to announce, that instead of that constant diminution of their numbers, produced by their wars and their wants, some of them begin to experience an increase of population.

[First Annual Message. December 8, 1801]

Brothers and friends of the Miamis, Powewatamies, and Weeauks:

I receive with great satisfaction the visit you have been so kind as to make us at this place, and I thank the Great Spirit who has conducted you to us in health and safety. It is well that friends should sometimes meet, open their minds mutually, and renew the chain of affection. Made by the same Great Spirit, and living in the same land with our brothers, the red men, we consider ourselves as of the same family; we wish to live with them as one people, and to cherish their interests as our own. The evils which of necessity encompass the live of man are sufficiently numerous. Why should we add to them by voluntarily distressing and destroying one another? Peace, brothers, is better than war. In a long and bloody war, we lose many friends, and gain nothing. Let us then live in peace and friendship together, doing to each other all the good we can. The wise and good on both sides desire this, and we must take care that the foolish and wicked among us shall not prevent it. On our part, we shall endeavor in all things to be just and generous towards you, and to aid you in meeting those difficulties which a change of circumstances is bringing on. We shall, with great pleasure, see your people become disposed to cultivate the earth, to raise herds of the useful animals, and to spin and weave, for their food and clothing. These resources are certain; they will never disappoint you: while those of hunting may fail, and expose your women and children to the miseries of hunger and cold. We will with pleasure furnish you with implements for the most necessary arts, and with persons who may instruct you how to make and use them.

[Washington, January 7, 1802]

The aboriginal inhabitants of these countries I have regarded with the commiseration their history inspires. Endowed with the faculties and the rights of men, breathing an ardent love of liberty and independence, and occupying a country which left them no desire but to be undisturbed, the stream of overflowing population from other regions directed itself on these shores; without power to divert, or habits to contend against, they have been overwhelmed by the current, or driven before it; now reduced within limits too narrow for the hunter's state, humanity enjoins us to teach them agriculture and the domestic arts; to encourage them to that industry which alone can enable them to maintain their place in existence, and to prepare them in time for that state of society, which to bodily comforts adds the improvement of the mind and morals.

We have therefore liberally furnished them with the implements of husbandry and household use; we have place among them instructors in the arts of first necessity; and they are covered with the aegis of the law against aggressors from among ourselves. But the endeavors to enlighten them on the fate which awaits their present course of life, to induce them to exercise their reason, follow its dictates, and change their pursuits with the change of circumstances, have powerful obstacles to encounter; they are combated by the habits of their bodies, prejudice of their minds, ignorance, pride, and the influence of interested and crafty individuals among them, who feel themselves something in the present order of things, and fear to become nothing in any other. These persons inculcate a sanctimonious reverence for the customs of their ancestors; that whatsoever they did, must be done through all time; that reason is a false guide, and to advance under its counsel, in their physical, moral or political condition, is perilous innovations; that their duty is to remain as their Creator made them, ignorance being safety, and knowledge full of danger; in short, my friends, among them is seen the action and counteractions of good sense and bigotry; they, too, have their anti-philosophers, who find an interest in keeping things in their present state, who dread reformation, and exert all their faculties to maintain the ascendancy of habit over the duty of improving our reason, and obeying its mandates.

[Second Inaugural Address. March 4, 1805]

My Friends and Children, Chiefly of the Cherokee Nation, Having now finished our business and finished it I hope to mutual satisfaction, I cannot take leave of you without expressing the satisfaction I have received from your visit. I see with my own eyes that the endeavors we have been making to encourage and lead you in the way of improving your situation have not been unsuccessful; it has been like grains sown in good ground, producing abundantly. You are becoming farmers, learning the use of the plough and the hoe, enclosing your grounds and employing that labor in their cultivation which you formerly employed in hunting and in war; and I see handsome specimens of cotton cloth raised, spun and wove by yourselves. You are also raising cattle and hogs for your food, and horses to assist your labors. Go on, my children, in the same way and be assured the further you advance in it the happier and more respectable you will be.

Our brethren, whom you have happened to meet here from the West and Northwest, have enabled you to compare your situation now with what it was formerly. they also make the comparison, and they see how far you are ahead of them, and seeing what you are they are encouraged to do as you have done. You will find your next want to be mills to grind your corn, which by relieving your women from the loss of time in beating it into meal, will enable them to spin and weave more. When a man has enclosed and improved his farm, builds a good house on it and raised plentiful stocks of animals, he will wish when he dies that these things shall go to his wife and children, whom he loves more than he does his other relations, and for whom he will work with pleasure during his life. You will, therefore, find it necessary to establish laws for this. When a man has property, learned by his own labor, he will not like to see another come and take it from him because he happens to be stronger, or else to defend it by spilling blood. You will find it necessary then to appoint good men, as judges, to decide contests between man and man, according to reason and to the rules you shall establish. If you wish to be aided by our counsel and experience in these things we shall always be ready to assist you with our advice.

My children, it is unnecessary for me to advise you against spending all your time and labor in warring with and destroying your fellow-men, and wasting your own members. You already see the folly and iniquity of it. Your young men, however, are not yet sufficiently sensible of it. Some of them cross the Mississippi to go and destroy people who have never done them an injury. My children, this is wrong and must not be; if we permit them to cross the Mississippi to war with the Indians on the other side of that river, we must let those Indians cross the river to take revenge on you. I say again, this must not be. The Mississippi now belongs to us. It must not be a river of blood. It is now the water-path along which all our people of Natchez, St. Louis, Indiana, Ohio, Tennessee, Kentucky and the western parts of Pennsylvania and Virginia are constantly passing with their property, to and from New Orleans. Young men going to war are not easily restrained. Finding our people on the river they will rob them, perhaps kill them. This would bring on a war between us and you. It is better to stop this in time by forbidding your young men to go across the river to make war. If they go to visit or to live with the Cherokees on the other side of the river we shall not object to that. That country is ours. We will permit them to live in it.

My children, this is what I wished to say to you. To go on in learning to cultivate the earth and to avoid war. If any of your neighbors injure you, our beloved men whom we place with you will endeavor to obtain justice for you and we will support them in it. If any of your bad people injure your neighbors, be ready to acknowledge it and to do them justice. It is more honorable to repair a wrong than to persist in it. Tell all your chiefs, your men, women and children, that I take them by the hand and hold it fast. That I am their father, wish their happiness and well-being, and am always ready to promote their good.

My children, I thank you for your visit and pray to the Great Spirit who made us all and planted us all in this land to live together like brothers that He will conduct you safely to your homes, and grant you to find your families and your friends in good health.

[Address to the Chiefs of the Cherokee Nation. Washington, January 10, 1806]

NATURAL LAW

The question, whether one generation of men has a right to bind another, seems never to have been started either on this or our side of the water. Yet it is a question of such consequences as not only to merit decision, but place also among the fundamental principles of every government. The course of reflection in which we are immersed here, on the elementary principles of society, has presented this question to my mind; and that no such obligation can be transmitted, I think very capable of proof. I set out on this ground, which I suppose to be self-evident, that the "earth belongs in usufruct to the living;" that the dead have neither powers nor rights over it. The portion occupied by any individual ceases to be his when himself ceases to be, and reverts to the society.

If the society has formed no rules for the appropriation of its lands in severalty, it will be taken by the first occupants, and these will generally be the wife and children of the descendent. If they have formed rules of appropriation, those rules may give it to the wife and children, or to some one of them, or to the legatee of the deceased. So they may give it to its creditor. But the child, the legatee or creditor, takes it, not by natural right but by a law of society of which he is a member, and to which he is subject. Then, no man can, by "natural right", oblige the lands he occupied, or the persons who succeed him in that occupation, to the payment of debts contracted by him. For if he could, he might during his own life, eat up the usufruct of the lands for several generations to come; and then the lands would belong to the dead, and not to the living, which is the reverse of our principle.

What is true of every member of the society, individually, is true of them all collectively; since the rights of the whole can be no more than the sum of the rights of the individuals. To keep our ideas clear when applying them to a multitude, let us suppose a whole generation of men to be born on the same day, to attain mature age on the same day, and to die on the same day, leaving a succeeding generation in the moment of attaining their mature age, all together. Let the ripe age be supposed of twenty-one years, and their period of life thirty-four years more, that being the average term given by the bills of mortality to persons of twenty-one years of age. Each successive generation would, in this way, come and go off the stage at a fixed moment, as individuals do now. Then I say, the earth belongs to each of these generations during its course, fully and in its own right. The second generation receives it clear of the debts and encumbrances of the first, the third of the second, and so on. For if the first could charge it with a debt, then the earth would belong to the dead and not to the living generation. Then, no generation can contract debts greater than may be paid during the course of its own existence.

The conclusion then, is, that neither the representatives of a nation, nor the whole nation itself assembled, can validly engage debts beyond what they may pay in their own time, that is to say, within thirty-four years of the date of the engagement.

With respect to future debts, would it not be wise and just for that nation to declare in the constitution they are forming, that neither the legislature nor the nation itself, can validly contract more debt than they may pay within their own age, or within the term of thirty-four years? And that all future contracts shall be deemed void, as to what shall remain unpaid at the end of thirty-four years from their date? This would put the lenders, and the borrowers also, on their guard. By reducing, too, the faculty of borrowing within its natural limits, it would bridle the spirit of war, to which too free a course has been procured by the inattention of money lenders to this law of nature, that succeeding generations are not responsible for the preceding.

On similar ground it may be proved, that no society can make a perpetual constitution, or even a perpetual law. The earth belongs always to the living generation: they may manage it, then, and what proceeds from it, as they please, during their usufruct. They are masters, too, of their own persons, and consequently may govern them as they please. But persons and property make the sum of the objects of government. The constitution and the laws of their predecessors are extinguished then, in their natural course, with those whose will gave them being. This could preserve that being, till it ceased to be itself, and no longer. Every constitution, then and every law, naturally expires at the end of thirty-four years. If it be enforced longer, it is an act of force, and not of right. It may be said, that the succeeding generation exercising, in fact, the power of repeal, this leaves them as free as if the constitution or law had been expressly limited to thirty-four years only. In the first place, this objection admits the right, in proposing an equivalent. But the power of repeal is not an equivalent. It might be, indeed, if every form of government were so perfectly contrived, that the will of the majority could always be obtained, fairly and without impediment. But this is true of no form. The people cannot assemble themselves; their representation is unequal and vicious. Various checks are opposed to every legislative proposition. Factions get possession of the public councils, bribery corrupts them, personal interests lead them astray from the general interests of their constitution; and other impediments arise, so as to prove to every practical man, that a law of limited duration is much more manageable than one which needs a repeal.

Turn this subject in your mind, my dear Sir, and particularly as to the power of contracting debts, and develop it with that cogent logic which is so peculiarly yours. Your station in the councils of our country gives you an opportunity of producing it to public consideration, of forcing it into discussion. At first blush it may be laughed at, as the dream of a theorist; but examination will prove it to be solid and salutary. It would furnish matter for a fine preamble to our first law for appropriating the public revenue; and it will exclude, at the threshold of our new government, the ruinous and contagious errors of this quarter of the globe, which have armed despots with means which nature does not sanction, for binding in chains their fellow-men. We have already given, in example, one effectual check to the dog of war, by transferring the power of declaring war from the executive to the legislative body, from those who are to spend, to those who are to pay. I should be pleased to see this second obstacle held out by us also, in the first instance. No nation can make a declaration against the validity of long-contracted debts, so disinterestedly as we, since we do not owe a shilling which will not be paid, principal and interest, by the measures you have taken, within the time of our own lives.

[Letter to James Madison. Paris, September 6, 1789]

The law of self-preservation overrules the laws of obligation in others. For the reality of these principles I appeal to the true fountains of evidence, the head and heart of every rational and honest man. It is there nature has written her moral laws, and where every man may read them for himself.

Questions of natural right are triable by their conformity with the moral sense and reason of man. Those who write treatises of natural law, can only declare what their own moral sense and reason dictate in the several cases they state. Such of them as happen to have feelings and a reason coincident with those of the wise and honest part of mankind, are respected and quoted as witnesses of what is morally right or wrong in particular cases. Grotius, Puffendorf, Wolf, and Vattel are of this number. Where they agree their authority is strong; but where they differ (and they often differ), we must appeal to our own feelings and reason to decide between them.

[Opinion on U.S. Treaties with France. April 28, 1793]

Every man, and every body of men on earth, possesses the right of self-government. They receive it with their being from the hand of nature. Individuals exercise it by their single will; collections of men by that of their majority; for the law of the majority is the natural law of every society of men. when a certain description of men are to transact together a particular business, the times and places of their meeting and separating, depend on their own will; they make a part of the natural right of self-government. This, like all other natural rights, may be abridged or modified in its exercise by their own consent, or by the law of those who depute them, if they meet in the right of others; but as far as it is not abridged or modified, they retain it as a natural right and may exercise them in what form they please, either exclusively by themselves, or in association with others, or by others altogether, as they shall agree.

[Opinion on moving government to the Potomac. July 15, 1790]

But our right is built on ground still broader and more unquestionable, to wit: On the law of nature and nations. If we appeal to this, as we feel it written on the heart of man, what sentiment is written in deeper characters than that the ocean is free to all men, and their rivers to all their inhabitants? Is there a man, savage or civilized, unbiased by habit, who does not feel and attest this truth?

Accordingly, in all tracts of country united under the same political society, we find this natural right universally acknowledged and protected by laying the navigable rivers open to all their inhabitants. When their rivers enter the limits of another society, if the right of the upper inhabitants to descend the stream is in any case obstructed, it is an act of force by a stronger society against a weaker, condemned by the judgment of mankind.

[Paper on the rights to navigate the Mississippi. March 18, 1792]

I consider the people who constitute a society or nation as the source of all authority in that nation; as free to transact their common concerns by any agents they think proper; to change these agents individually, or the organization of them in form or function whenever they please; that all the acts done by these agents under the authority of the nation, are the acts of the nation, are obligatory to them and inure to their use, and can in no wise be annulled or affected by any change in the form of government, or of the persons administering it, consequently the treaties between the United States and France, were not treaties between the United States and France, were not treaties between the United States and Louis Capet, but between the two nations of America and France; and the nations remaining in existence, though both of them have since changed their forms of government, the treaties are not annulled by these changes. The law of nations, by which this question is to be determined, is composed of three branches. 1. The moral law of our nature. 2. The usage's of nations. 3. Their special conventions.

The first of these only concerns this question, that is to say the moral law to which man has been subjected by his creator, and of which his feelings or conscience, as it is sometimes called, are the evidence with which his creator has furnished him. The moral duties which exist between individual and individual in a state of nature, accompany them into a state of society, and the aggregate of the duties of all the individuals composing the society constitutes the duties of that society towards any other; so that between society and society the same moral duties exist as did between the individuals composing them, while in an unassociated state, and their maker not having released them from those duties on their forming themselves into a nation. Compacts then, between nation and nation, are obligatory on them by the same moral law which obliges individuals to observe their compacts.

There are circumstances, however, which sometimes excuse the non-performance of contracts between man and man; so are there also between nation and nation. When performance, for instance, becomes impossible, non-performance is not immoral; so if performance becomes self-destructive to the party, the law of self-preservation overrules the laws of obligation in others.

For the reality of these principles I appeal to the true fountains of evidence, the head and heart of every rational and honest man. It is there nature has written her moral laws, and where every man may read them for himself. He will never read there the permission to annul his obligations for a time, or forever, whenever they become dangerous, useless, or disagreeable; certainly not when merely useless or disagreeable...and though he may, under certain degrees of danger, yet the danger must be imminent, and the degree great. Of these, it is true, that nations are to be judges for themselves; since no one nation has a right to sit in judgment over another; but the tribunal of our conscience remains, and that also of the opinion of the world. These will revise the sentence we pass in our own case, and as we respect these, we must see that in judging ourselves we have honestly done the part of impartial and rigorous judges.

[Opinion on U.S. Treaties with France. April 28, 1793]

Can one generation bind another, and all others, in succession forever? I think no. The Creator has made the earth for the living, not the dead. Rights and powers can only belong to persons, not to things, not to mere matter, unendowed with will. The dead are not even things. The particles of matter which composed their bodies, make part now of the bodies of other animals, vegetables, or minerals, of a thousand forms. To what then are attached the rights and powers they held while in the form of men? A generation may bind itself as long as its majority continues in life; when that has disappeared, another majority is in place, holds all the rights and powers their predecessors once held, and may change their laws and institutions to suit themselves. Nothing then is unchangable but the inherent and unalienable rights of man.

[Letter to Major John Cartwright. Monticello, June 5, 1814]

OPINION

I never had an opinion in politics or religion, which I was afraid to own. A costive reserve on these subjects might have procured me more esteem from some people, but less from myself.

[Letter to Francis Hopkinson. Paris, March 13, 1789]

Subject opinion to coercion: whom will you make your inquisitors? Fallible men; men governed by bad passions, by private as well as public reasons. And why subject it to coercion? To produce uniformity. But is uniformity of opinion desirable? No more than of face and stature. Introduce the bed of Procrustes then, and as there is danger that the large men may beat the small, make us all of a size, by lopping the former and stretching the latter. Difference of opinion is advantageous in religion. The several sects perform the office of a "censor morum" over such other. Is uniformity attainable? Millions of innocent men, women, and children, since the introduction of Christianity, have been burnt, tortured, fined, imprisoned; yet we have not advanced one inch towards uniformity. What has been the effect of coercion? To make one half the world fools, and the other half hypocrites.

[Notes on Virginia]

During the contest of opinion through which we have passed, the animation of discussion and of exertions has sometimes worn an aspect which might impose on strangers unused to think freely and to speak and to write what they think; but this being now decided by the voice of the nation, announced according to the rules of the constitution, all will, of course, arrange themselves under the will of the law, and unite in common efforts for the common good.

[**Inauguration Address. March 4, 1801**]

But every difference of opinion is not a difference of principle. We have called by different names brethren of the same principle. We are all republicans we are federalists. If there be any among us who would wish to dissolve this Union or to change its republican form, let them stand undisturbed as monuments of the safety with which error of opinion may be tolerated where reason is left free to combat it.

[**Inauguration Address. March 4, 1801**]

POLITICAL PARTIES

For in truth, the parties of Whig and Tory, are those of nature. They exist in all countries, whether called by these names, or by those of Aristocrats and Democrats, Cote' Droite and Cote' Gauche, Ultras and Radicals, Serviles and Liberals. The sickly, weakly, timid man, fears the people, and is a Tory by nature. The healthy, strong and bold, cherishes them, and is formed a Whig by nature.

[Letter to the Marquis de Lafayette. Monticello, November 4, 1823]

I am not a federalist, because I never submitted the whole system of my opinions to the creed of any party of men whatever, in religion, in philosophy, in politics or in anything else, where I was capable of thinking for myself. Such an addiction, is the last degradation of a free and moral agent. If I could not go to heaven but with a party, I would not go there at all. Therefore, I am not of the party of federalists. But I am much farther from that of the anti-federalists.

[Letter to Francis Hopkinson. Paris, March 13, 1789]

I am no believer in the amalgamation of parties, nor do I consider it as either desirable or useful for the public; but only that, like religious differences, a difference in politics should never be permitted to enter into social intercourse, or to disturb its friendships, its charities, or justice. In that form, they are censors of the conduct of each other, and useful watchmen for the public. Men by their constitutions are naturally divided into two parties: 1. Those who fear and distrust the people, and wish to draw all powers from them into the hands of the higher classes. 2. Those who identify themselves with the people, have confidence in them, cherish and consider them as the most honest and safe, although not the most wise depository of the public interests. In every country these two parties exist, and in every one where they are free to think, speak, and write, they will declare themselves.

[Letter to Henry Lee. Monticello, August 10, 1824]

POWER

An honest man can feel no pleasure in the exercise of power over his fellow citizens. And considering as the only offices of power those conferred by the people directly, that is to say, the executive and legislative functions of the General and State governments, the common refusal of these, and multiplied resignations, are proofs sufficient that power is not alluring to pure minds, and is not, with them, the primary principle of contest. This is my belief of it; it is that on which I have acted; and had it been a mere contest who should be permitted to administer the government according to its genuine republican principles, there has never been a moment of my life in which I should have relinquished for it the enjoyments of my family, my farm, my friends and books.

[Letter to John Melish. Monticello, January 13, 1813]

PRESIDENCY

I know the difficulty of obtaining belief to one's declarations of a disinclination to honors, and that it is greatest with those who still remain in the world. But no arguments were wanting to reconcile me to a relinquishment of the first office or acquiescence under the second. As to the first it was impossible that a more solid unwillingness settled on full calculation, could have existed in any man's mind, short of the degree of absolute refusal. The only view on which I would have gone into it for awhile was to put our vessel on her republican tack before she should be thrown too much to leeward of her true principles. As to the second, it is the only office in the world about which I am unable to decide in my own mind whether I had rather have it or not have it. Pride does not enter into the estimate; for I think with the Romans that the general of to-day should be a soldier to-morrow if necessary.

[Letter to James Madison. Monticello, January 1, 1797]

The second office of the government is honorable and easy, the first is but a splendid misery.

[Letter to Elbridge Gerry. Philadelphia, May 13, 1797]

PRESTIGE

Your letter had kindled all the fond recollections of ancient times; recollections much dearer to me than anything I have known since. There are minds which can be pleased by honors and preferments; but I see nothing in them but envy and enmity. It is only necessary to possess them, to know how little they contribute to happiness, or rather how hostile they are to it. No attachments soothe the mind so much as those contracted in early life; nor do I recollect any societies which have given me more pleasure, than those of which you have partaken with me. I had rather be shut up in a very modest cottage, with my books, my family and a few old friends, dining on simple bacon, and letting the world roll on as it liked, than to occupy the most splendid post, which any human power can give.

[Letter to Mr. Alexander Donald. Paris, February 7, 1788]

PRINCIPLES OF GOVERNMENT

About to enter, fellow citizens, on the exercise of duties which comprehend everything dear and valuable to you, it is proper that you should understand what I deem the essential principles of our government, and consequently those which ought to shape its administration. I will compress them within the narrowest compass they will bear, stating the general principle, but not all its limitations.

Equal and exact justice to all men, of whatever state or persuasion, religious or political; peace, commerce, and honest friendship, with all nations—entangling alliances with none; the support of the state governments in all their rights, as the most competent administrations for our domestic concerns and the surest bulwarks against anti-republican tendencies; the preservation of the general government in its whole constitutional vigor, as the sheet anchor of our peace at home and safety abroad; a jealous care of the right of election by the people—a mild and safe corrective of abuses which are lopped by the sword of the revolution where peaceable remedies are unprovided; absolute acquiescence in the decisions of the majority the vital principle of republics, from which there is no appeal but to force, the vital principle and immediate parent of despotism; a well-disciplined militia—our best reliance in peace and for the first moments of war, till regulars may relieve them; the supremacy of the civil over the military authority; economy in the public expense, that labor may be lightly burdened; the honest payment of our debts and sacred preservation of the public faith; encouragement of agriculture, and of commerce as its handmaiden; the diffusion of information and the arraignment of all abuses at the bar of public reason; freedom of religion; freedom of the press; freedom of person under the protection of the habeas corpus; and trial by juries impartially selected—these principles form the bright constellation which has gone before us, and guided our steps through an age of revolution and reformation.

The wisdom of our sages and the blood of our have been devoted to their attainment. They should be the creed of our political faith—the text of civil instruction the touchstone by which to try the services of those we trust; and should we wander from them in moments of error or alarm, let us hasten to retrace our steps and to regain the road which alone leads to peace, liberty, and safety.

[Inauguration Address. March 4, 1801]

On taking this station on a former occasion, I declared the principles on which I believed it my duty to administer the affairs of our commonwealth. My conscience tells me that I have, on every occasion, acted up to that declaration, according to its obvious import, and to the understanding of every candid mind.

[Second Inaugural Address. March 4, 1805]

PUBLIC SERVICE

If we are made in some degree for others, yet, in a greater, are we made for ourselves. It were contrary to feeling, and indeed ridiculous to suppose that a man had less rights in himself than one of his neighbors, or indeed all of them put together. This would be slavery, and not that liberty which the bill of rights has made inviolable, and for the preservation of which our government has been charged. Nothing could so completely divest us of that liberty as the establishment of the opinion, that the State has a perpetual right to the services of all its members. This, to men of certain ways of thinking, would be to annihilate the blessings of existence, and to contradict the Giver of life, who gave it for happiness and not for wretchedness. And certainly, to such it were better that they had never been born.

However, with these, I may think public service and private misery inseparably linked together. I have not the vanity to count myself among those whom the State would think worth oppressing with perpetual service. I have received a sufficient momento to the contrary. I am persuaded that, having hitherto dedicated to them the whole of the active and useful part of my life, I shall be permitted to pass the rest in mental quiet. I hope, too, that I did not mistake modes any more than the matter of right when I preferred a simple act of renunciation, to the taking sanctuary under those disqualifications (provided by the law for other purposes indeed but) affording asylum also for rest to the wearied. I dare say you did not expect by the few words you dropped on the right of renunciations to expose yourself to the fatigue of so long a letter, but I wished you to see that, if I had done wrong, I had been betrayed by a semblance of right at least.

[Letter to Colonel James Monroe. Monticello, May 20th, 1782]

It is now more than a year that I have withdrawn myself from public affairs, which I never liked in my life, but was drawn into by emergencies which threatened our country with slavery, but ended in establishing it free. I have returned with infinite appetite, to the enjoyment of my farm, my family and my books, and had determined not to meddle in nothing beyond their limits.

[Letter to Monsieur D'Ivernois. Monticello, February 6, 1795]

REASON

In fact, it is comfortable to see the standard of reason at length erected, after so many ages, during which the human mind has been held in vassalage by kings, priests, and nobles; and it is honorable for us, to have produced the first legislature who had the courage to declare, that the reason of man may be trusted with the formation of his own opinions.

[Letter to James Madison from Paris, December 16, 1786]

In a republican nation, whose citizens are to be led by reason and persuasion, and not by force, the art of reasoning becomes of first importance.

[Letter to Mr. David Harding. Monticello, April 20, 1824]

Reason and free inquiry are the only effectual agents against error.

[Notes on Virginia]

Reason and experiment have been indulged, and error has fled before them. It is error alone which needs the support of government. Truth can stand by itself.

[**Notes on Virginia**]

REBELLIONS

Can history produce an instance of rebellion so honorably conducted? I say nothing of its motives. They were founded in ignorance, not wickedness. God forbid we should ever be twenty years without such a rebellion. The people cannot be all, and always, well informed. The part which is wrong will be discontented, in proportion to the importance of the facts they misconceive. If they remain quiet under such misconceptions, it is a lethargy, the forerunner of death to the public liberty. We have had thirteen states independent for eleven years. There has been one rebellion. That comes to one rebellion in a century and a half, for each State. What country before ever existed a century and a half without a rebellion? And what country can preserve its liberties, if its rulers are not warned from time to time, that this people preserve the spirit of resistance? Let them take arms. The remedy is to set them rights as to facts, pardon and pacify them. What signify a few lives lost in a century or two? The tree of liberty must be refreshed from time to time, with the blood of patriots and tyrants. It is its natural manure.

[Letter to Colonel William Stephens Smith. Paris, November 3, 1787]

Even this evil [rebellion] is productive of good. It prevents the degeneracy of government, and nourishes a general attention to the public affairs. I hold it, that a little rebellion, now and then, is a good thing, and as necessary in the political world as storms in the physical. Unsuccessful rebellions, indeed, generally establish the encroachments on the rights of the people, which have produced them. An observation of this truth should render honest republican governors so mild in their punishment of rebellions, as not to discourage them too much. It is a medicine necessary for the sound health of government.

[Letter to James Madison. Paris, January 30, 1787]

Go on then in doing with your pen what in other times was done with the sword: show that reformation is more practicable by operating on the mind than on the body of man.

[Letter to Thomas Paine. Philadelphia, June 19, 1792]

RELIGION

The declaration, that religious faith shall be unpunished, does not give impunity to criminal acts, dictated by religious error.

[Letter to James Madison. Paris, July 31, 1788]

I never submitted the whole system of my opinions to the creed of any party of men whatever, in religion, in philosophy, in politics or in anything else, where I was capable of thinking for myself. Such an addiction, is the last degradation of a free and moral agent. If I could not go to heaven but with a party, I would not go there at all.

[Letter to Francis Hopkinson. Paris, March 13, 1789]

In matters of religion, I have considered that its free exercise placed by the constitution independent of the powers of the general government. I have therefore undertaken, on no occasion, to prescribe the religious exercises suited to it; but have left them, as the constitution found them, under the direction and discipline of State or Church authorities acknowledged by the several religious societies.

[Second Inaugural Address. March 4, 1805]

I am for freedom of religion, and against all maneuvers to bring about a legal ascendancy of one sect over another.

[**Letter to Elbridge Gerry. Philadelphia, January 26, 1799**]

This is a summary view of that religious slavery under which a people have been willing to remain, who have lavished their lives and fortunes for the establishment of their civil freedom. The error seems not sufficiently eradicated, that the operations of the mind, as well as the acts of the body, are subject to the coercion of the laws. But our rulers can have no authority over such natural rights, only as we have submitted to them. The rights of conscience we never submitted, we could not submit. We are answerable for them to our God. The legitimate powers of government extend to such acts only as are injurious to others. But it does me no injury for my neighbor to say there are twenty gods, or no God. It neither picks my pocket nor breaks my leg. If it be said, his testimony in a court of justice cannot be relied on, reject it then, and be the stigma on him. Constraint may make him worse by making him a hypocrite, but it will never make him a truer man. It may fix him obstinately in his errors, but will not cure them. Reason and free inquiry are the only effectual agents against error. Give a loose to them, they will support the true religion by bringing every false one to their tribunal, to the test of their investigation. They are the natural enemies of error, and of error only. Had not the Roman government permitted free inquiry, Christianity could never have been introduced. Had not free inquiry been indulged at the era of the Reformation, the corruptions of Christianity could not have been purged away. If it be restrained now, the present corruptions will be protected, and new ones encouraged. Was the government to prescribe to us our medicine and diets, our bodies would be in such keeping as our souls are now.

[Notes on Virginia]

And let us reflect that having banished from our land that religious intolerance as despotic, as wicked, and capable of as bitter and bloody persecutions. During the throes and convulsions of the ancient world, during the agonizing spasm of infuriated man, seeking through blood and slaughter his long-lost liberty, it was not wonderful that the agitations of the billows should reach even this distant and peaceful shore; that this should be more felt and feared by some and less by others; that this should divide opinions as to measures of safety.

[Inauguration Address. March 4, 1801]

Religion. Your reason is now mature enough to examine this object. In the first place, divest yourself of all bias in favor of novelty and singularity of opinion. Indulge them in any other subject rather than that of religion. It is too important, and the consequences of error may be too serious. On the other hand, shake off all the fears and servile prejudices, under which weak minds are servilely crouched. Fix reason firmly in her seat, and call to her tribunal every fact, every opinion. Question with boldness even the existence of a God; because, if there be one, he must more approve of the homage of reason, than that of blindfolded fear. You will naturally examine first, the religion of your own country. Read the Bible, then, as you would read Livy or Tacitus. the facts which are within the ordinary course of nature, you will believe on the authority of the writer, as you do those of the same kind in Livy and Tacitus. The testimony of the writer weighs in their favor, in one scale, and their not being against the laws of nature, does not weigh against them. But those facts in the Bible which contradict the laws of nature, must be examined with more care, and under a variety of faces. Here you must recur to the pretensions of the writer to inspiration from God. Examine upon what evidence his pretensions are founded, and whether that evidence is so strong, as that its falsehood would be more improbable than a change in the laws of nature, in the case he relates. For example, in the book of Joshua, we are told, the sun stood still several hours. Were we to read that fact in Livy or Tacitus, we should class it with their showers of blood, speaking of statues, beasts, etc. But it is said, that the writer of that book was inspired. Examine, therefore, candidly, what evidence there is of his having been inspired. The pretension is entitled to your inquiry, because millions believe it. On the other hand, you are astronomer enough to know how contrary it is to the law of nature that a body revolving on its axis, as the earth does, should have stopped, should not, by that sudden stoppage, have prostrated animals, trees, buildings, and should after a certain time have resumed its revolution, and that without a second general prostration. Is this arrest of the earth's motion, or the evidence which affirms it, most with the law of probabilities? You will next read the New Testament. It is the history of a personage called Jesus. Keep in your eye the opposite pretensions: 1, of the who say he was begotten by God, born of a virgin, suspended and reversed the laws of nature at will, and ascended bodily into heaven; and 2, of those who say he was a man of illegitimate birth, of a benevolent heart, enthusiastic mind, who set out without pretensions to divinity, ended in believing them, and was punished capitally for sedition, by being gibbeted, according to the Roman law, which punished the first commission of that offence by whipping, and the second by exile, or death "in furea"....

Do not be frightened from this inquiry by any fear of its consequences. If it ends in a belief that there is no God, you will find incitements to virtue in the comfort and pleasantness you feel in its exercise, and the love of others which it will procure you. If you find reason to believe there is a God, a consciousness that you are acting under his eye, and that he approves you, will be a vast additional incitement; if that there be a future state, the hope of a happy existence in that increases the appetite to deserve it; if that Jesus was also a God, you will be comforted by a belief of his aid and love. In fine, I repeat, you must lay aside all prejudice on both sides, and neither believe nor reject anything, because any other persons, or descriptions of persons, have rejected or believed it. Your own reason is the only oracle given you by heaven, and you are answerable, not for the rightness, but uprightness of the decision. I forgot to observe, when speaking of the New Testament, that you should read all the histories of Christ, as well of those whom a council of ecclesiastics have decided for us, to be Pseudo-evangelists, as those they named Evangelists. Because those Pseudo-evangelist pretended to inspiration, as much as the others, and you are to judge their pretensions by your own reason, and not by the reason of those ecclesiastics. Most of these are lost. There are some, however, still extant, collected by Fabricius, which I will endeavor to get and send you.

[**Letter to Peter Carr. Paris, August 10, 1787**]

The delusion into which the X.Y.Z. plot showed it possible to push the people; the successful experiment made under the prevalence of that delusion on the clause of the Constitution, which, while it secure the freedom of the press, covered also the freedom of religion, had given to the clergy a very favorite hope of obtaining an establishment of a particular form of Christianity through the United States; and as every sect believes its own form the true one, every one perhaps hoped for his own, but especially the

Episcopalians and Congregationalists. The returning good sense of our country threatens abortion to their hopes, and they believe that any portion of power confided to me, will be exerted in opposition to their schemes. And they believe rightly: for I have sworn upon the altar of God, eternal hostility against every form of tyranny over the mind of man.

[Letter to Dr. Benjamin Rush. Monticello, September 23, 1800]

In some of the delightful conversations with you, in the evenings of 1798-99, and which served as an anodyne to the afflictions of the crisis through which our country was then laboring, the Christian religion was sometimes our topic; and I then promised you, that one day or other, I would give you my views of it. They are the result of a life of inquiry and reflection, and very different from that anti-Christian system imputed to me by those who know nothing of my opinions. To the corruptions of Christianity I am, indeed, opposed; but not to the genuine precepts of Jesus himself. I am a Christian, in the only sense in which he wished any one to be; sincerely attached to his doctrines, in preference to all others; ascribing to himself every "human" excellence; and believing he never claimed any other.

I am moreover averse to the communication of my religious tenets to the public; because it would countenance the presumption of those who have endeavored to draw them before that tribunal, and to seduce public opinion to erect itself into that inquisition over the rights of conscience, which the laws have so justly prescribed. It behooves every man who values liberty of conscience for himself, to resist invasions of it in the case of others; or their case may, by change of circumstances, become his own. It behooves him, too, in his own case, to give no example of concession, betraying the common right of independent opinion, by answering questions of faith, which the laws have left between God and himself.

[Letter to Doctor Benjamin Rush. Washington, April 21, 1803]

RELIGIOUS FREEDOM

Well aware that Almighty God hath created the mind free; that all attempts to influence it by temporal punishments or burdens, or by civil incapacitations, tend only to beget habits of hypocrisy and meanness, and are a departure from the plan of the Holy Author of our religion, who being Lord both of body and mind, yet chose not to propagate it by coercions on either, as was in his Almighty power to do; that the impious presumption of legislators and rulers, civil as well as ecclesiastical, who, being themselves but fallible and uninspired men have assumed dominion over the faith of others, setting up their own opinions and modes of thinking as the only true and infallible, and as such endeavoring to impose them on others, hath established and maintained false religions over the greatest part of the world, and through all time; that to compel a man to furnish contributions of money for the propagation of opinions which he disbelieves, is sinful and tyrannical; that even the forcing him to support this or that teacher of his own religious persuasion, is depriving him of the comfortable liberty of giving his contributions to the particular pastor whose morals he would make his pattern, and whose powers he feels most persuasive to righteousness, and is withdrawing from the ministry those temporal rewards, which proceeding from an approbation of their personal conduct, are an additional incitement to earnest and unremitting labors for the instruction of mankind; that our civil rights have no dependence on our religious opinions, more than our opinions in physics or geometry; that, therefore, the proscribing any citizen as unworthy the public confidence by laying upon him an incapacity of being called to the offices of trust and emolument, unless he profess or renounce this or that religious opinion, is depriving him injuriously of those privileges and advantages to which in common with his fellow citizens he has a natural right; that it tends also to corrupt the principles of that very religion it is meant to encourage, by bribing, with a monopoly of worldly honors and emoluments, those who will externally profess and conform to it; that though indeed these are criminal who not withstand such temptation, yet neither are those innocent who lay the bait in their way; that to suffer the civil magistrate to intrude his powers into the field of opinion and to restrain the profession or propagation of principles, on the supposition of their ill tendency, is a dangerous fallacy, which at once destroys all religious liberty, because he being of course judge of that tendency, will make his opinions the rule of judgment, and approve or condemn the sentiments of others only as they shall square with or differ from his own; that it is time enough for the rightful purposes of civil government, for its offices to interfere when principles break out into overt acts against peace and good order; and finally, that truth is great and will prevail if left to herself, that she is the proper and sufficient antagonist to error, and has nothing to fear from the conflict, unless by human interposition disarmed of her natural weapons, free argument and debate, errors ceasing to be dangerous when it is permitted freely to contradict them. "Be it therefore enacted by the General Assembly", That no man shall be compelled to frequent or support any religious worship, place or ministry whatsoever, nor shall be enforced, restrained, molested, or burthened in his body or goods, nor shall otherwise suffer on account of his religious opinions or belief; but that all men shall be free to profess, and by argument to maintain, their opinions in matters of religion, and that the same shall in nowise diminish, enlarge, or affect their civil capacities. And though we well know this Assembly, elected by the people for the ordinary purposes of legislation only, have no power to restrain the acts of succeeding assemblies, constituted with the powers equal to our own, and that therefore to declare this act irrevocable, would be of no effect in law, yet we are free to declare, and do declare, that the rights hereby asserted are of the natural rights of mankind, and that if any act shall be hereafter passed to repeal the present or to narrow its operation, such act will be an infringement of natural right.

[The Virginia Statute for Religious Freedom]

I am really mortified to be told that, "in the United States of America", a fact like this can become a subject of inquiry, and of criminal inquiry too, as an offence against religion; that a question about the sale of a book can be carried before the civil magistrate. Is this then our freedom of religion? and are we to have a censor whose imprimatur shall say what books may be sold, and what we may buy? And who is thus to dogmatize religious opinions for our citizens? Whose foot is to be the measure to which ours are all to be cut or stretched? Is a priest to be our inquisitor, or shall a layman, simple as ourselves, set up his reason as the rule for what we are to read, and what we must believe? It is an insult to our citizens to question whether they are rational beings or not, and blasphemy against religion to suppose it cannot stand the test of truth and reason. If M. de Becourt's book be false in its facts, disprove them; if false in its reasoning, refute it. But for God's sake, let us freely hear both sides, if we choose.

[Letter to Monsieur N.G. Dufief. Monticello, April 19, 1814]

REPUBLIC

You have successfully and completely pulverized Mr. Adams' system of
orders, and his opening the mantle of republicanism to every government
of laws, whether consistent or not with natural right. Indeed, it must be
acknowledged, that the term "republic" is of very vague application in
every language. Witness the self-styled republics of Holland, Switzerland,
Genoa, Venice, Poland. Were I to assign to this term a precise and definite
idea, I would say, purely and simply, it means a government by its citizens
in mass, acting directly and personally, according to rules established by
the majority; and that every other government is more or less republican,
in proportion as it has in its composition more or less of this ingredient of
the direct action of the citizens.

Such a government is evidently restrained to very narrow limits of space
and population. I doubt if it would be practicable beyond the extent of a
New England township. The first shade from this pure element, which,
like that of pure vital air, cannot sustain life of itself, would be where the
powers of the government, being divided, should be exercised each by representatives chosen either "pro hac vice", expressing the will of their constituents. This I should consider as the nearest approach to a pure
republic, which is practicable on a large scale of country or population.
And we have examples of it in some of our State Constitutions, which, if
not poisoned by priest-craft, would prove its excellence over all mixtures
with other elements; and, with only equal doses of poison, would still be
the best.

Other shades of republicanism may be found in other forms of government, where the executive, judiciary and legislative functions, and the different branches of the latter, are chosen by the people more or less directly, for longer terms of years, or for life, or made hereditary; or where there are mixtures of authorities, some dependent on, and others independent of the people. The further the departure from direct and constant control by the citizens, the less has the government of the ingredient of republicanism; evidently none where the authorities are hereditary, as in France, Venice, etc., or self-chosen, as in Holland; and little, where for life, in proportion as the life continues in being after the act of election.

The purest republican feature in the government of our own State, is the House of Representatives. The Senate is equally so the first year, less the second, and so on. The Executive still less, because not chosen by the people directly. The Judiciary seriously anti-republican, because for life; and the national arm wielded, as you observe, by military leaders, irresponsible but to themselves. Add to this the vicious constitution of our county courts (to whom the justice, the executive administration, the taxation, police, the military appointments of the county, and nearly all our daily concerns are confided), self-appointed, self-continued, holding their authorities for life, and with an impossibility of breaking in on the perpetual succession of any faction once possessed of the bench. They are in truth, the executive, the judiciary, and the military of their respective counties, and the sum of the counties makes the State. And add, also, that one-half of our brethren who fight and pay taxes, are excluded, like Helots, from the rights of representation, as if society were instituted for the soil, and not for the men inhabiting it; or one-half of these could dispose of the rights and the will of the other half, with their consent.

In the General Government, the House of Representatives is mainly republican; the Senate scarcely so at all, as not elected by the people directly, and so long secured even against those who do elect them; the Executive more republican than the Senate, from its shorter term, its election by the people, in "practice", (for they vote for A only on an assurance that he will vote for B,) and because, "in practice also", a principle of rotation seems to be in a course of establishment; the judiciary independent of the nation, their coercion by impeachment being found nugatory. If, then, the control of the people over the organs of their government be the measure of its republicanism, and I confess I know no other measure, it must be agreed that our governments have much less of republicanism than ought to have been expected; in other words, that the people have less regular control over their agents, than their rights and their interests require. And this I ascribe, not to any want of republican dispositions in those who formed these Constitutions, but to a submission of true principle to European authorities, to speculators on government, whose fears of the people have been inspired by the populace of their own great cities, and were unjustly entertained against the independent, the happy, and therefore orderly citizens of the United States.

Much I apprehend that the golden moment is past for reforming these heresies. The functionaries of public power rarely strengthen in their dispositions to abridge it, and an unorganized call for timely amendment is not likely to prevail against an organized opposition to it. We are always told that things are going on well; why change them? "Chista bene, non si muove," said the Italian, "let him who stands well, stand still." This is true; and I verily believe they would go on well with us under an absolute monarch, while our present character remains, of order, industry and love of peace, and restrained, as he would be, by the proper spirit of the people. But it is while it remains such, we should provide against the consequences of its deterioration. And let us rest in the hope that it will yet be done, and spare ourselves the pain of evils which may never happen. On this view of the import of the term "republic", instead of saying, as has been said, "that it may mean anything or nothing," we may say with truth and meaning, that governments are more or less republican, as they have more or less of the element of popular election and control in their composition; and believing, as I do, that the mass of the citizens is the safest depository of their own rights and especially, that the evils flowing from the duperies of the people, are less injurious than those from the egoism of their agents, I am a friend to that composition of government which has in it the most of this ingredient. And I sincerely believe, with you, that banking establishments are more dangerous than standing armies; and that the principle of spending money to be paid by posterity, under the name of funding, is but swindling futurity on a large scale.

[Letter to John Taylor. Monticello, May 28, 1816]

The first principle of republicanism is, that the "lex majoris partis" is the fundamental law of every society of individuals of equal rights; to consider the will of the society enounced by the majority of a single vote, as sacred as if unanimous, is the first of all lessons in importance, yet the last which is thoroughly learnt. this law once disregarded, no other remains but that of force, which ends necessarily in military depotism.

[Letter to Baron Alexander von Humboldt. Monticello, June 13, 1817]

RETIREMENT

Within a few days I retire to my family, my books and farms; and having gained the harbor myself, I shall look on my friends still buffeting the storm with anxiety indeed, but not with envy. Never did a prisoner, released from his chains, feel such relief as I shall on shaking off the shackles of power. Nature intended me for the tranquil pursuits of science, by rendering them my supreme delight. But the enormities of the times in which I have lived, have forced me to take a part in resisting them, and to commit myself on the boisterous ocean of political passions. I thank God for the opportunity of retiring from them without censure, and carrying with me the most consoling proofs of public approbation. I leave everything in the hands of men so able to take care of them, that if we are destined to meet misfortunes, it will be because no human wisdom could avert them. Should you return to the United States, perhaps your curiosity may lead you to visit the hermit of Monticello. He will receive you with affection and delight; hailing you in the meantime with his affectionate salutations and assurances of constant esteem and respect.

P.S. If you return to us, bring a couple of pair of true-bred shepherd's dogs. You will add a valuable possession to a country now beginning to pay great attention to the raising sheep.

[Letter to Monsieur DuPont de Nemours. Washington, March 2, 1809]

Returning to the scenes of my birth and early life, to the society of those with whom I was raised, and who have been ever dear to me, I receive, fellow citizens and neighbors, with inexpressible pleasure, the cordial welcome you are so good as to give me. Long absent on duties which the history of a wonderful era made incumbent on those called to them, the pomp, the turmoil, the bustle and splendor of office, have drawn but deeper sighs for the tranquil and irresponsible occupations of private life, for the enjoyment of an affectionate intercourse with you, my neighbors and friends, and the endearments of family love, which nature has given us all, as the sweetener of every hour. For these I gladly lay down the distressing burden of power, and seek, with my fellow citizens, repose and safety under the watchful cares, the labors and perplexities of younger and abler minds. The anxieties you express to administer to my happiness, do, of themselves, confer that happiness; and the measure will be complete, if my endeavors to fulfil my duties in the several public stations to which I have been called, have obtained for me the approbation of my country. The part which I have acted on the theatre of public life, has been before them; and to their sentence I submit it; but the testimony of my native county, of the individuals who have known me in private life, to my conduct in its various duties and relations, is the more grateful, as proceeding from eye witnesses and observers, from triers of the vicinage. Of you, then, my neighbors, I may ask, in the fact of the world, "whose ox have I taken, or whom have I defrauded: Whom have I oppressed, or of whose hand have I received a bribe to blind mine eyes therewith?" On your verdict I rest with conscious security. You wishes for my happiness are received with just sensibility, and I offer sincere prayers for your own welfare and prosperity.

[Letter to the Inhabitants of Albemarle County. Monticello, April 3, 1809]

I am retired to Monticello, where, in the bosom of my family, and sur-rounded by my books, I enjoy a repose to which I have been long a stranger. My mornings are devoted to correspondence. From breakfast to dinner, I am in my shops, my garden, or on horseback among my farms; from dinner to dark, I give to society and recreation with my neighbors and friends; and from candle light to early bed-time, I read. My health is perfect; and my strength considerably reinforced by the activity of the course I pursue; perhaps it is as great as usually falls to the lot of near sixty-seven years of age. I talk of ploughs and harrows, of seeding and harvest-ing, with my neighbors, and of politics too, if they choose, with as little reserve as the rest of my fellow citizens, and feel, at length, the blessing of being free to say and do what I please, without being responsible for it to any mortal. A part of my occupation, and by no means the least pleasing, is the direction of the studies of such young men as ask it. They place themselves in the neighboring village, and have the use of my library and counsel, and make a part of my society. In advising the course of their reading, I endeavor to keep their attention fixed on the main objects of all science, the freedom and happiness of man. So that coming to bear a share in the councils and government of their country, they will ever in view the sole objects of all legitimate government.

[Letter to General Thaddeus Kosciusko. Monticello, February 26, 1810]

My present course of life admits less reading than I wish. From breakfast, or noon at latest, to dinner, I am mostly on horseback, attending to my farm or other concerns, which I find healthful to my body, mind and affairs; and the few hours I can pass in my cabinet, are devoured by corre-spondences; not those with my intimate friends, with whom I delight to interchange sentiments, but with others, who, writing to me on concerns of their own in which I have had an agency, or from motives of mere respect and approbation, are entitled to be answered with respect and a return of good will. My hope is that this obstacle to the delights of retirement, will wear away with the oblivion which follows that, and that I may at length be indulged in those studious pursuits, from which nothing but revolutionary duties would ever have called me.

[Letter to Dr. Benjamin Rush. Monticello, January 16, 1811]

RIGHTS

The error seems not sufficiently eradicated, that the operations of the mind, as well as the acts of the body, are subject to the coercion of the laws. But our rulers can have no authority over such natural rights, only as we have submitted to them. The rights of conscience we never submitted, we could not submit. We are answerable for them to our God. The legitimate powers of government extend to such acts only as are injurious to others.

[**Notes on Virginia**]

But is the spirit of the people an infallible, a permanent reliance? Is it government? Is this the kind of protection we receive in return for the rights we give up? Besides, the spirit of the times may alter, will alter. Our rulers will become corrupt, our people careless. A single zealot may commence persecutor, and better men be his victims. It can never be too often repeated, that the time for fixing every essential right on a legal basis is while our rules are honest, and ourselves united. From the conclusion of this war we shall be going down hill. It will not then be necessary to resort every moment to the people for support. They will be forgotten, therefore, and their rights disregarded. They will forget themselves, but in the sole faculty of making money, and will never think of uniting to effect a due respect for their rights. The shackles, therefore, which shall not be knocked off at the conclusion of this war, will remain on us long, will be made heavier and heavier, till our rights shall revive or expire in a convulsion.

[Notes on Virginia]

The public mind is manifestly advancing on the abusive prerogatives of their governors, and bearing them down. No force in the government can withstand this, in the long run. Courtiers had rather give up power than pleasures; they will barter, therefore, the usurped prerogatives of the King, for the money of the people. This is the agent by which modern nations will recover their rights.

[Letter to the Count De Moustier. Paris, May 17, 1788]

There are rights which it is useless to surrender to the government, and which governments have yet always been found to invade. These are the rights of thinking, and publishing our thoughts by speaking or writing; the right of free commerce; the right of personal freedom. There are instruments for administering the government, so peculiarly trust-worthy, that we should never leave the legislature at liberty to change them. The new Constitution has secured these in the executive and legislative depart-ment; but not in the judiciary. It should have established trials by the peo-ple themselves, that is to say, by jury. There are instruments so dangerous to the rights of the nation, and which place them so totally at the mercy of their governors, that those governors, whether legislative or executive, should be restrained from keeping such instruments on foot, but in well-defined cases. Such an instrument is a standing army. We are now allowed to say, such a declaration of rights, as a supplement to the Constitution where that is silent, is wanting, to secure us in these points.

[Letter to Colonel Humphreys. Paris, March 18, 1789]

SCIENCE

I trust, that with your dispositions, even the acquisition of science is a pleasing employment. I can assure you, that the possession of it is, what (next to an honest heart) will above all things render you dear to your friends, and give you fame and promotion in your own country. When your mind shall be well improved with science, nothing will be necessary to place you in the highest points of view, but to pursue the interests of your country, the interests of your friends, and your own interests also, with the purest integrity, the most chaste honor.

[Letter to Peter Carr. Paris, August 19, 1785]

I have received a copy of the evidence at large respecting the discovery of the vaccine inoculation which you have been pleased to send me, and for which I return you my thanks. Having been among the early converts, in this part of the globe, to its efficiency, I took an early part in recommending it to my countrymen. I avail myself of this occasion of rendering you a portion of the tribute of gratitude due to you from the whole human family. Medicine has never before produced any single improvement of such utility. Harvey's discovery of the circulation of the blood was a beautiful addition to our knowledge of the animal economy, but on a review of the practice of medicine before and since that epoch, I do not see any great amelioration which has been derived from that discovery. You have erased from the calendar of human afflictions one of its greatest. Yours is the comfortable reflection that mankind can never forget that you have lived. Future nations will know by history only that the loathsome small-pox has existed and by you has been extirpated. Accept my fervent wishes for your health and happiness and assurances of the greatest respect and consideration.

[**Letter to the Reverend Doctor G. C. Jenner. Monticello, May 14, 1806**]

But even in Europe a change has sensibly taken place in the mind of man. Science had liberated the ideas of those who read and reflect, and the American example had kindled feelings of right in the people. An insurrection has consequently begun, of science, talents, and courage, against rank and birth, which have fallen into contempt. It has failed in its first effort, because the mos of the cities, the instrument used for its accomplishment, debased by ignorance, poverty, and vice, could not be restrained to rational action. But the world will recover from the panic of this first catastrophe. Science is progressive, and talents and enterprise on the alert. Resort may be had to the people of the country, a more governable power from their principles and subordination; and rank, and birth, and tinsel-aristocracy will finally shrink into insignificance, even there. This, however, we have no right to meddle with. It suffices for us, if the moral and physical condition of our own citizens qualifies them to select the able and good for the direction of their government, with a recurrence of elections at such short periods as will enable them to displace an unfaithful servant, before the mischief he meditates may be irremediable.

[**Letter to John Adams. Monticello, October 28, 1813**]

When I contemplate the immense advances in science and discoveries in the arts which have been made within the period of my life, I look forward with confidence to equal advances by the present generation, and have no doubt they will consequently be as much wiser than we have been as we than our fathers were, and they than the burners of witches.

[Letter to Dr. Benjamin Waterhouse. Monticello, March 3, 1818]

SELF-GOVERNMENT

A sense of necessity, and a submission to it, is to me a new and consolatory proof that, whenever the people are well-informed, they can be trusted with their own government; that, whenever things get so far wrong as to attract their notice, they may be relied on to set them to rights.

[Letter to Dr. Price. Paris, November 18, 1788]

When you witnessed our first struggles in the War of Independence, you little calculated, more than we did, on the rapid growth and prosperity of this country; on the practical demonstration it was about to exhibit, of the happy truth that man is capable of self-government, and only rendered otherwise by the moral degradation designedly super-induced on him by the wicked acts of his tyrants. I have much confidence that we shall proceed successfully for ages to come, and that, contrary to the principle of Montesquieu, it will be seen that the larger the extent of country, the more firm its republican structure, if founded, not on conquest, but in principles of compact and equality. My hope of its duration is build much on the enlargement of the resources of life going hand in hand with the enlargement of territory, and the belief that men are disposed to live honestly, if the means of doing so are open to them.

[Letter to Monsieur Barbe de Marbois. Monticello, June 14, 1817]

SIN TAX

A tax on whiskey is to discourage its consumption; a tax on foreign spirits encourages whiskey by removing its rival from competition. The price and present duty throw foreign spirits already out of competition with whiskey, and accordingly they are used but to a salutary extent. You see no persons besotting themselves with imported spirits, wines, liquors, cordials, etc. Whiskey claims to itself alone the exclusive office of sot-making. Foreign spirits, wines, teas, coffee, sugars, salt, are articles of as innocent consumption as broadcloths and silks; and ought, like them, to pay but the average "ad valorem" duty of other imported comforts. All of them are ingredients in our happiness, and the government which steps out of the ranks of the ordinary articles of consumption to select and lay under disproportionate burdens a particular one, because it is a comfort, pleasing to the taste, or necessary to health, and will therefore be bought, is, in that particular, a tyranny.

[Letter to General Samuel Smith. Monticello, May 3, 1823]

STATES RIGHTS

When we consider that this government is charged with the external and mutual relations only of these states; that the states themselves have principal care of our persons, our property, and our reputation, constituting the great field of human concerns, we may well doubt whether our organization is not too complicated, too expensive; whether offices and officers have not been multiplied unnecessarily, and sometimes injurious to the service they were meant to promote.

[First Annual Message. December 8, 1801]

It is not enough that honest men are appointed Judges. All know the influence of interest on the mind of man, and how unconsciously his judgement is warped by that influence. To this bias add that of the "esprit de corps", of their peculiar maxim and creed, that "it is the office of a good Judge to enlarge his jurisdiction," and the absence of responsibility; and how can we expect impartial decision between the General government, of which they are themselves so eminent a part, and an individual State, from which they have nothing to hope or fear? We have seen, too, that contrary to all correct example, they are in the habit of going out of the question before them, to throw an anchor ahead, and grapple further hold for future advances of power. They are then, in fact, the corps of sappers and miners, steadily working to under mine the independent rights of the States, and to consolidate all power in the hands of the government in which they have so important a freehold estate. But it is not by the consolidation, or concentration of powers, but by their distribution, that good government is effected.

[**Autobiography of Thomas Jefferson**]

The line of division now, is the preservation of State rights, as reserved in the Constitution, or by strained constructions of that instrument, to merge all into a consolidated government. The Tories are for strengthening the Executive and General Government; the Whigs cherish the representative branch, and the rights reserved by the States, as the bulwark against consolidation, which must immediately generate monarch.

[**Letter to the Marquis de Lafayette. Monticello, November 4, 1823**]

I am for preserving to the States the powers not yielded by them to the Union, and to the legislature of the Union it constitutional share in the division of powers; and I am not for transferring all the powers of the States to the General Government, and all those of the government to the executive branch.

[**Letter to Elbridge Gerry. Philadelphia, January 26, 1799**]

TAXATION

At home, fellow citizens, you best know whether we have done well or ill. The suppression of unnecessary offices, of useless establishments and expenses, enabled us to discontinue our internal taxes. These covering our land with officers, and opening our doors to their intrusions, had already begun that process of domiciliary vexation which, once entered, is scarcely to be restrained from reaching successively every article of produce and property. If among these taxes some minor ones fell which had not been inconvenient, it was because their amount would not have paid the officers who collected them, and because, if they had any merit, the state authorities might adopt them, instead of others less approved.

The remaining revenue on the consumption of foreign articles, is paid cheerfully by those who can afford to add foreign luxuries to domestic comforts, being collected on our seaboards and frontiers only, and incorporated with the transactions of our mercantile citizens, it may be the pleasure and pride of an American to ask, what farmer, what mechanic, what laborer, ever sees a tax gatherer of the United States? These contributions enable us to support the current expenses of the government, to fulfill contracts with foreign nations, to extinguish the native right of soil within our limits, to extend those limits, and to apply such a surplus to our public debts, as places at a short day their final redemption, and that redemption once effected, the revenue thereby liberated may, by a just repartition among the states, and a corresponding amendment of the constitution, be applied, "in time of peace", to rivers, canals, roads, arts, manufactures, education, and other great objects within each state. "In time of war", if injustice, by ourselves or others, must sometimes produce war, increased as the same revenue will be increased by population and consumption, and aided by other resources reserved for that crisis, it may meet within the year all the expenses of the year, without encroaching on the rights of future generations, by burdening them with the debts of the past.

[**Second Inaugural Address. March 4, 1805**]

TERM LIMITS

The second amendment which appears to me essential is the restoring the principle of necessary rotation, particularly to the Senate and Presidency: but most of all to the last. Re-eligibility makes him an officer for life, and the disasters inseparable from an elective monarchy, render it preferable if we cannot tread back that step, that we should go forward and take refuge in an hereditary one. Of the correction of this article, however, I entertain no present hope, because I find it has scarcely excited an objection in America. And if it does not take place ere long, it assuredly never will.

[Letter to Colonel Carrington. Paris, May 27, 1788]

The abandoning the principle of necessary rotation in the Senate, has, I see, been disapproved by many; in the case of the President, by none. I readily, therefore, suppose my opinion wrong, when opposed by the majority, as in the former instance, and the totality, as in the latter.

[Letter to James Madison. Paris, July 31, 1788]

If some termination to the services of the chief magistrate be not fixed by the Constitution, or supplied by practice, his office, nominally for years, will in fact become for life; and history shows how easily that degenerates into an inheritance. Believing that a representative government, responsible at short periods of election, is that which produces the greatest sum of happiness to mankind, I feel it a duty to do no act which shall essentially impair that principle; and I should unwillingly be the person who, disregarding the sound precedent set by an illustrious predecessor, should furnish the first example of prolongation beyond the second term of office.

[To the General Assembly of North Carolina. Washington, January 10, 1808]

TRADE

Whenever jealousies are expressed as to any supposed view of ours, on the dominion of the West Indies, you cannot go farther than the truth, in asserting we have none. If there be one principle more deeply rooted than any other in the mind of every American, it is, that we should have nothing to do with conquest. As to commerce, indeed, we have strong sensations. In casting our eyes over the earth, we see no instance of a nation forbidden, as we are, by foreign powers, to deal with neighbors, and obliged, with them, to carry into another hemisphere, the mutual supplies necessary to relieve mutual wants. This is not merely a question between the foreign power and our neighbor. We are interested in it equally with the latter, and nothing to moderation, at least with respect to us, can render us indifferent to its continuance. An exchange of surpluses and wants between neighbor nations, is both a right and a duty under the moral law, and measures against right should be mollified in their exercise, if it be wished to lengthen them to the greatest term possible.

[Letter to William Short. Philadelphia, July 28, 1791]

As to commerce, two methods occur. 1. By friendly arrangements with the several nations with whom these restrictions exist: Or, 2. By the separate act of our own legislatures for countervailing their effects. There can be no doubt but that of these two, friendly arrangement is the most eligible. Instead of embarrassing commerce under piles of regulating laws, duties and prohibitions, could it be relieved from all its shackles in all parts of the world, could every country be employed in producing that which nature has best fitted it to produce, and each be free to exchange with others mutual surpluses for mutual wants, the greatest mass possible would then be produced of those things which contribute to human life and human happiness; the numbers of mankind would be increased, and their condition bettered.

But should any nation, contrary to our wishes, suppose it may better find its advantage by continuing its system of prohibitions, duties, and regulations, it behooves us to protect our citizens, their commerce and navigation, by counter prohibitions, duties and regulations, also. Free commerce and navigation are not to be given in exchange for restrictions and vexations; nor are they likely to produce a relaxation of them.

Where a nation imposes high duties on our productions, or prohibits them altogether, it may be proper for us to do the same by theirs; first burdening or excluding those productions which they bring here, in competition with our own of the same kind; selecting next, such manufactures as we take from them in greatest quantity, and which, at the same time, we could the soonest furnish to ourselves, or obtain from other countries; imposing on them duties lighter at first, but heavier and heavier afterwards as other channels of supply open.

Such duties having the effect of indirect encouragement to domestic manufactures of the same kind, may induce the manufacturer to come himself into these States, where cheaper subsistence, equal laws, and a vent of his wares, free of duty, may ensure him the highest profits from his skill and industry. And here, it would be in the power of the State governments to co-operate essentially, by opening the resources of encouragement which are under their control, extending them liberally to artists in those particular branches of manufacture for which their soil, climate, population and other circumstances have matured them, and fostering the precious efforts and progress of household manufacture, by some patronage suited to the nature of its objects, guided by the local informations they possess, and guarded against abuse by their presence and attentions. The oppressions on our agriculture, in foreign ports, would thus be made the occasion of relieving it from a dependence on the councils and conduct of others, and of promoting arts, manufactures and population at home.

[Report on the privileges and restrictions on the commerce of the United States in foreign countries. December 16, 1793]

In general, it is a truth that if every nation will employ itself in what it is fittest to produce, a greater quantity will be raised of the things contributing to human happiness, than if every nation attempts to raise everything it wants with itself.

[Letter to Monsieur Lasteyrie. Washington, July 15, 1808]

WAR AND PEACE

I confess to you I have seen enough of one war never to wish to see another.

[Letter to John Adams. Monticello, April 25, 1794]

The evils which of necessity encompass the life of man are sufficiently numerous. Why should we add to them by voluntarily distressing and destroying one another? Peace, brothers, is better than war. In a long and bloody war, we lose many friends, and gain nothing. Let us then live in peace and friendship together, doing to each other all the good we can. The wise and good on both sides desire this, and we must take care that the foolish and wicked among us shall not prevent it.

[Address to the Miamis, Powtewatamies, and Weeauks. Washington, January 7, 1802]

We have seen with sincere concern the flames of war lighted up again in Europe, and nations with which we have the most friendly and useful relations engaged in mutual destruction. While we regret the miseries in which we see others involved, let us bow with gratitude to the kind Providence which, inspiring with wisdom and moderation our late legislative councils while placed under the urgency of the greatest wrongs, guarded us from hastily entering into the sanguinary contest, and left us only to look on and to pity its ravages. These will be heaviest on those immediately engaged. Yet the nations pursuing peace will not be exempt from all evil.

In the course of this conflict, let it be our endeavor, as it is our interest and desire, to cultivate the friendship of the belligerent nations by every act of justice and of incessant kindness; to receive their armed vessels with hospitality from the distresses of the sea, but to administer the means of annoyance to none; to establish in our harbors such a police as may maintain law and order; to restrain our citizens from embarking individually in a war in which their country takes no part; to punish severely those persons, citizen or alien, who shall usurp the cover of our flag for vessels not entitled to it, infecting thereby with suspicion those of real Americans, and committing us into controversies for the redress of wrongs not our own; to exact from every nation the observance, toward our vessels and citizens, of those principles and practices which all civilized people acknowledge; to merit the character of a just nation, and maintain that of an independent one, preferring every consequence to insult and habitual wrong.

Separated by a wide ocean from the nations of Europe, and from the political interests which entangle them together, with productions and wants which render our commerce and friendship useful to them and theirs to us, it cannot be the interest of any to assail us, nor ours to disturb them. We should be most unwise, indeed, were we to cast away the singular blessings of the position in which nature has placed us, the opportunity she has endowed us with of pursuing, at a distance from foreign contentions, the paths of industry, peace, and happiness; of cultivating general friendship, and of bringing collisions of interest to the umpirage of reason rather than of force.

[Third Presidential Annual Message. October 17, 1803]

We are alarmed here with the apprehensions of war; and sincerely anxious it may be avoided; but not at the expense with of our faith or honor. It seems much the general opinion here, the latter has been too much wounded not to require reparation, and to seek it even in war, if that be necessary. As to myself, I love peace, and I am anxious that we should give the world still another useful lesson, by showing to them other modes of punishing injuries by war, which is as much a punishment to the punisher as to the sufferer. I love, therefore,...[the] proposition of cutting off all communication with the nation which has conducted itself so atrociously. This, you will say, may bring on war. If it does, we will meet it like men; but it may not bring on war, and then the experiment will have been a happy one. I believe this war would be vastly more unanimously approved than any one we ever were engaged in; because the aggressions have been so wanton and bare-faced, and so unquestionably against our desire.

[Letter to Tench Coxe. Monticello, May 1, 1794]

All men know that war is a losing game to both parties. But they know also that if they do not resist encroachment at some point, all will be taken from them, and that more would then be lost even in dollars and cents by submission than resistance. It is the case of giving a part to save the whole, a limb to save life. If is the melancholy law of human societies to be com-pelled sometimes to choose a great evil in order to ward off a greater; to deter their neighbors from rapine by making it cost them more than hon-est gains.

[Letter to William Short, Esq. Monticello, November 28, 1814]

WELFARE

The poor unable to support themselves, are maintained by an assessment on the tytheable persons in their parish. This assessment is levied and administered by twelve persons in each parish, called vestrymen, originally chosen by the housekeepers of the parish, but afterwards filling vacancies in their own body by their own choice. These are usually the most discreet farmers, so distributed through their parish, that every part of it may be under the immediate eye of some one of them. They are well acquainted with the details and economy of private life, and they find sufficient inducements to execute their charge well, in their philanthropy, in the approbation of their neighbors, and the distinction which that gives them.

The poor who have neither property, friends, nor strength to labor, are boarded in the houses of good farmers, to whom a stipulated sum is annually paid. To those who are able to help themselves a little, or have friends from whom they derive some succors, inadequate however to their full maintenance, supplementary aids are given which enable them to live comfortably in their own houses, or in the houses of their friends. Vagabonds without visible property or vocations, are placed in work houses, where they are well clothed, fed, lodged and made to labor. Nearly the same method of providing for the poor prevails through all our States; and from Savannah to Portsmouth you will seldom meet a beggar. In the large towns, indeed, they sometimes present themselves. These are usually foreigners, who have never obtained a settlement in any parish. I never yet saw a native American begging in the streets or highways. A subsistence is easily gained here; and if, by misfortunes, they are thrown on the charities of the world, those provided by their own country are so comfortable and so certain, that they never think of relinquishing them to become strolling beggars.

[Notes on Virginia]

I think it fortunate for the United States to have become the asylum for so many virtuous patriots of different denominations: but their circumstances, with which you were so well acquainted before, enabled them to be but a bare asylum, and to offer nothing for them but an entire freedom to use their own means and faculties as they please.

[Letter to M. de Meusnier. Monticello, Virginia, April 29, 1795]

ADVICE TO THE YOUNG

It is your future happiness which interests me, and nothing can contribute more to it (moral rectitude always excepted) than the contracting a habit of industry and activity. Of all the cankers of human happiness none corrodes with so silent, yet so baneful a tooth, as indolence. Body and mind both unemployed, our being becomes a burden, and every object about us loathsome, even the dearest. Idleness begets ennui, ennui the hypochondria, and that a diseased body. No laborious person was ever yet hysterical. Exercise and application produce order in our affairs, health of body, cheerfulness of mind, and these make us precious to our friends.

It is while we are young that the habit of industry is formed. If not then, it never is afterwards. The fortune of our lives, therefore, depends on employing well the short period of youth. If at any moment, my dear, you catch yourself in idleness, start from it as you would from the precipice of a gulf. You are not, however, to consider yourself as unemployed while taking exercise. That is necessary for your health, and health is the first of all objects. For this reason, if you leave your dancing-master for the summer, you must increase your other exercise. I do not like your saying that you are unable to read the ancient print of your Livy, but with the aid of your master. We are always equal to what we undertake with resolution. A little degree of this will enable you to decipher your Livy. If you always lean on your master, you will never be able to proceed without him.

It is part of the American character to consider nothing as desperate<@151>to surmount every difficulty by resolution and contrivance. In Europe there are shops for every want: its inhabitants therefore have no idea that their wants can be furnished otherwise. Remote from all other aid, we are obliged to invent and to execute; to find means within ourselves, and not to lean on others. Consider, therefore, the conquering your Livy as an exercise in the habit of surmounting difficulties; a habit which will be necessary to you in the country where you are to live, and without which you will be thought a very helpless animal, and less esteemed.

Music, drawing, books, invention, and exercise, will be so many resources to you against ennui. But there are others which, to this object, add that of utility. These are the needle and domestic economy. The latter you cannot learn here, but the former you may. In the country life of America there are many moments when a woman can have recourse to nothing but her needle for employment. In a dull company and in dull weather, for instance, it is ill manners to read; it is ill manners to leave them; no card-playing there among genteel people that is abandoned to blackguards. The needle is then a valuable resource. Besides, without knowing how to use it herself, how can the mistress of a family direct the works of her servants?

You ask me to write you long letters. I will do it, my dear, on condition you will read them from time to time, and practice what they will inculcate. Their precepts will be dictated by experience, by a perfect knowledge of the situation in which you will be placed, and by the fondest love for you. This it is which makes me wish to see you more qualified than common. My expectations from you are high yet not higher than you may attain. Industry and resolution are all that are wanting.

Nobody in this world can make me so happy, or so miserable, as you. Retirement from public life will ere long become necessary for me. To your sister and yourself I look to render the evening of my life serene and contented. Its morning has been clouded by loss after loss, till I have nothing left but you. I do not doubt either your affection or dispositions. But great exertions are necessary, and you have little time left to make them. Be industrious, then, my dear child. Think nothing insurmountable by resolution and application and you will be all that I wish you to be.

[**Letter to Martha Jefferson. Aix-en Provence, March 28, 1787**]

Give about two of them [hours], every day, to exercise; for health must not be sacrificed to learning. A strong body makes the mind strong. As to the species of exercise, I advise the gun. While this gives a moderate exercise to the body, it gives boldness, enterprise, and independence to the mind. Games played with the ball, and others of that nature, are too violent for the body, and stamp no character on the mind. Let your gun, therefore, be the constant companion of your walks. Never think of taking a book with you. The object of walking is to relax the mind. You should therefore not permit yourself even to think while you walk; but divert yourself by the objects surrounding you. Walking is the best possible exercise. Habituate yourself to walk very far.

The Europeans value themselves on having subdued the horse to the uses of man; but I doubt whether we have not lost more than we have gained, by the use of this animal. No one has occasioned so much the degeneracy of the human body. An Indian goes on foot nearly as far in a day, for a long journey, as an enfeebled white does on his horse; and he will tire the best horses. There is no habit you will value so much as that of walking far without fatigue. I would advise you to take your exercise in the afternoon; not because it is the best time for exercise, for certainly it is not; but because it is the best time to spare from your studies; and habit will soon reconcile it to health, and render it nearly as useful as if you gave to that the more precious hours of the day. A little walk of half an hour, in the morning, when you first rise, is advisable also. It shakes off sleep, and produces other good effects in the animal economy. Rise at a fixed and an early hour, and go to bed at a fixed and early hour also. Sitting up late at night is injurious to the health, and not useful to the mind.

[Letter to Peter Carr.<@151>Paris, August 19, 1785]

I have received letters which inform me that our dear Polly will certainly come to us this summer. By the time I return, it will be time to expect her. When she arrives, she will become a precious charge on your hands. The difference of your age, and your common loss of a mother, will put that office on you. Teach her to be always true; no vice is so mean as the want of truth, and at the same time so useless. Teach her never to be angry: Anger only serves to torment ourselves, to divert others, and alienate their esteem. And teach her industry and application to useful pursuits. I will venture to assure you, that if you inculcate this in her mind, you will make her a happy being herself, a most inestimable friend to you, and precious to all the world. In teaching her these dispositions of mind, you will be more fixed in them yourself, and render yourself dear to all your acquaintances. Practice them, then, my dear, without ceasing. If ever you find yourself in difficulty, and doubt how to extricate yourself, do what is right, and you will find it the easiest way of getting out of the difficulty. Do it for the additional incitement of increasing the happiness of him who loves you infinitely,

[Letter to Martha Jefferson.<@151>Toulon, April 7, 1787]

A determination never to do what is wrong, prudence and good humor, will go far towards securing to you the estimation of the world. When I recollect that at fourteen years of age, the whole care and direction of myself was thrown on myself entirely, without a relation or friend qualified to advise or guide me, and recollect the various sorts of bad company with which I associated from time to time, I am astonished I did not turn off with some of them, and become as worthless to society as they were. I had the good fortune to become acquainted very early with some characters of very high standing, and to feel the incessant wish that I could ever become what they were. Under temptations and difficulties, I would ask myself what would Dr. Small, Mr. Wythe, Peyton Randolph do in this situation? What course in it will insure me their approbation?

I am certain that this mode of deciding on my conduct, tended more to correctness than any reasoning powers I possessed. Knowing the even and dignified line they pursued, I could never doubt for a moment which of two courses would be in character for them. Whereas, seeking the same object through a process of moral reasoning, and with the jaundiced eye of youth, I should often have erred.

From the circumstances of my position, I was often thrown into the society of horse racers, card players, fox hunters, scientific and professional men, and of dignified men; and many a time have I asked myself, in the enthusiastic moment of the death of a fox, the victory of a favorite horse, the issue of a question eloquently argued at the bar, or in the great council of the nation, well, which of these kinds of reputation should I prefer? That of a horse jockey? a fox hunter? an orator? or the honest advocate of my country's rights? Be assured, my dear Jefferson, that these little returns into ourselves, this self-catechising habit, is not trifling nor useless, but leads to the prudent selection and steady pursuit of what is right.

I have mentioned good humor as one of the preservatives of our peace and tranquility. It is among the most effectual, and its effect is so well imitated and aided, artificially, by politeness, that this also becomes an acquisition of first rate value. In truth, politeness is artificial good humor, it covers the natural want of it, and ends by rendering habitual a substitute nearly equivalent to the real virtue. It is the practice of sacrificing to those whom we meet in society, all the little conveniences and preferences which will gratify them, and deprive us of nothing worth a moment's consideration; it is the giving a pleasing and flattering turn to our expressions, which will conciliate others, and make them pleased with us as well as themselves. How cheap a price for the good will of another! When this is in return for a rude thing said by another, it brings him to his senses, it mortifies and corrects him in the most salutary way, and places him at the feet of your good nature, in the eyes of the company.

But in stating prudential rules for our government in society, I must not omit the important one of never entering into dispute or argument with another. I never saw an instance of one of two disputants convincing the other by argument. I have seen many, on their getting warm, becoming rude, and shooting one another. Conviction is the effect of our own dispassionate reasoning, either in solitude, or weighing within ourselves, dispassionately, what we hear from others, standing uncommitted in argument ourselves. It was one of the rules which, above all others, made Doctor Franklin the most amiable of men in society, 'never to contradict anybody'. If he was urged to announce an opinion, he did it rather by asking questions, as if for information, or by suggesting doubts. When I hear another express an opinion which is not mine, I say to myself, he has a right to his opinion, as I to mine; why should I question it? His error does me no injury, and shall I become a Don Quixote, to bring all men by force of argument to one opinion?

If a fact be misstated, it is probably he is gratified by a belief of it, and I have no right to deprive him of the gratification. If he wants information, he will ask it, and then I will give it in measured terms; but if he still believes his own story, and shows a desire to dispute the fact with me, I hear him and say nothing. It is his affair, not mine, if he prefers error.

There are two classes of disputants most frequently to be me with among us. The first is of young students, just entered the threshold of science, with a first view of its outlines, not yet filled up with the details and modification which a further progress would bring to their knowledge. The other consists of the ill-tempered and rude men in society, who have taken up a passion for politics. (Good humor and politeness never introduce into mixed society, a question of which they foresee there will be a difference of opinion.) From both of these classes of disputants, my dear Jefferson, keep aloof, as you would from the infected subjects of yellow fever or pestilence. Consider yourself, when with them, as among the patients of Bedlam, needing medical more than moral counsel. Be a listener only, keep within yourself, and endeavor to establish with yourself the habit of silence, especially on politics. In the fevered state of our country, no good can ever result from any attempt to set one of these fiery zealots to rights, either in fact or principle. They are determined as to the facts they will believe, and the opinions on which they will act. Get by them, therefore, as you would by an angry bull; it is not for a man of sense to dispute the road with such an animal. You will be more exposed than others to have these animals shaking their horns at you, because of the relation in which you stand with me.

Full of political venom, and willing to see me and to hate me as a chief in the antagonist party, you presence will be to them what the vomit grass is to the sick dog, a nostrum for producing ejaculation. Look upon them exactly with that eye, and pity them as objects to whom you can administer only occasional ease. My character is not within their power. It is in the hands of my fellow citizens at large, and will be consigned to honor or infamy by the verdict of the republican mass of our country, according to what themselves will have seen, not what their enemies and mine shall have said. Never, therefore, consider these puppies in politics as requiring any notice from you, and always show that you are not afraid to leave my character to the umpirage of public opinion. Look steadily to the pursuits which have carried you to Philadelphia, be very select in the society you attach yourself to, avoid taverns, drinkers, smokers, idlers, and dissipated persons generally; for it is with such that broils and contentions arise; and you will find your path more easy and tranquil. The limits of my paper warn me that it is time for me to close with my affectionate adieu.

[Letter to Thomas Jefferson Randolph.<@151>Washington, November 24, 1808]

This letter will, to you, be as one from the dead. The writer will be in the grave before you can weight its counsels. Your affectionate and excellent father has requested that I would address to you something which might possibly have a favorable influence on the course of life you have to run, and I too, as a namesake, feel an interest in that course. Few words will be necessary, with good dispositions on your part. Adore God. Reverence and cherish your parents. Love your neighbor as yourself, and your country more than yourself. Be just. Be true. Murmur not at the ways of Providence. So shall the life into which you have entered, be the portal to one of eternal and ineffable bliss. And if to the dead it is permitted to care for the things of this world, every action of your life will be under my regard. Farewell.

A Decalogue of Canons for observation in practical life

1. Never put off till to-morrow what you can do to-day.

2. Never trouble another for what you can do yourself.

3. Never spend your money before you have it.

4. Never buy what you do not want, because it is cheap; it will be dear to you.

5. Pride costs us more than hunger, thirst, and cold.

6. We never repent of having eaten too little.

7. Nothing is troublesome that we do willingly.

8. How much pain have cost us the evils which have never happened.

9. Take things always by their smooth handle.

10. When angry, count ten, before you speak; if very angry, an hundred.

[Letter to Thomas Jefferson Smith. Monticello, February 21, 1825]

www.ingramcontent.com/pod-product-compliance
Lightning Source LLC
Chambersburg PA
CBHW061408280526
45784CB00001B/405